Qualtrics Survey Software

Handbook for Research Professionals

2nd Edition

Official Training Guide from Qualtrics

ISBN: 978-0-9849328-0-1
© 2013 Qualtrics Labs Inc.

BY QUALTRICS ENGINEERING AND CREATIVE TEAMS

Published by
Qualtrics Labs, Inc.
2250 N. University Parkway #48C
Provo, Utah, 84604, USA
+1.801.374.6682

Website Address
www.Qualtrics.com

Table of Contents

Introduction 06

Chapter 1: Create and Manage Surveys 07
Creating Your First Survey 08
The Create Survey Tab 09
  Quick Survey Builder 10
  Create From Copy 10
  Survey Library 11
Navigating the My Surveys Tab 11
  Task Icons 11
  Collaboration 13
Show More Data 16
Organizing More Surveys 17
  Sort by Heading 17
  Folders 17
  Search 18
  Renaming Surveys 18
Research Suite Helps 19

Chapter 2: Your Account Libraries 21
Navigate Your Libraries 22
  Survey Library 23
  Question Library 24
  Graphics Library 24
  Files Library 25
  Message Library 26

Chapter 3: Edit Your Survey 29
Add and Position Questions 30
  Adding Questions with the Green "+" Buttons 30
  Copy Questions From 31
  Copy Question 31
  Move Question 31
  Preview Questions 32

Add a Page Break 33
Edit Questions 34
  Selecting a Question Type 34
  Editing Text 34
  Edit Answer Choices 36
  Allow Text Entry 36
  Rich Content Editor for Answer Choices 37
  Insert Graphic 38
  Exclude From Analysis 38
  Insert Piped Text 39
  Add Display Logic to an Answer Choice 39
  Move Up and Move Down 40
  Remove Choice 40
  Validation 41
  Force Response 41
  Request Response 41
  Content Type Validation 41
  Custom Validation 42
Look and Feel 43
  Skins 43
  General Tab 44
  Fonts Tab 45
  Colors Tab 45
  Advanced Tab 46
Survey Options 47
  Survey Experience 48
  Survey Protection 49
  Survey Termination 50
  Inactive Surveys 50
  Partial Completion 51
  Response Set 52
Spell Check 52
Preview Survey 53
Print Survey 54

Chapter 4: Advanced Question Options 57

  Advanced Question Options Button 58

    Add Display Logic .... 59 .

    Carry Forward Choices 60

    Add Skip Logic 61

    Add JavaScript 62

    Add Default Choices 63

    Recode Values 64

    Randomization 65

    Choice Groups.. 67

  Additional Question Options 68

    Survey Preview Mode 68

    Strip Formatting 68

    Auto-Number Questions 68

    Check Survey Accessibility 69

Chapter 5: Block Options and Survey Flow .. 73

  Blocks and Block Options 74

    Question Blocks 74

    Add and Delete a Block 75

    Block Options 75

    View Block 76

    Collapse Questions 76

    Lock Block.. 77

    Question Randomization Within a Block 77

    Loop & Merge 79

    Loop & Merge Over Question Response............ 79

    Static Loop & Merge 81

    Move Block Up 82

    Move Block Down 82

    Copy Block 83

    Copy Block to Library 83

    Delete Block 83

  Survey Flow 84

    Handling the Survey Elements 85

    How to Use the Survey Flow Elements 87

    Branch 87

    Embedded Data 88

    Embedded Data in the Survey Flow 88

    Randomizer 90

    Evenly Present Elements 90

    Web Service 91

    Authenticator 92

    End of Survey 93

    Table of Contents.. 95

    Conjoint 96

Chapter 6: Special Features 99

  Triggers 100

    Email Triggers 100

    Panel Triggers 102

  Salesforce 103

    Web to Lead 104

    Response Mapping to Salesforce 106

    Trigger and Email Survey 107

    To Pass Embedded Data from Salesforce

    to Qualtrics 109

    Qualtrics on Salesforce App Exchange 109

  Quotas 110

  Conjoint Analysis 112

  Translate Survey 115

  Scoring 116

  Test Survey 118

  Import Survey 118

    Importing a Text File 120

  Export Survey 123

    Export Survey to Word 123

Chapter 7: Distribute Survey 125

  Distribute Survey Tab 126

    Survey Link 126

    Email Survey 127

    Email History 130

    Send Reminder or Thank You 131

    Social Media 131

    In-Page Popup 133

    Website Feedback 134

    Survey Director 135

Chapter 8: Panels 139

The Panels Tab 140

Add Panel Members 141

Panel Actions 142

Panel Members 144

Update Panel Members 145

Import From a Survey 146

Miscellaneous Panel Member Tasks 147

Sample Management 148

Chapter 9: View Results 151

View Reports 152

Create New Reports 152

Folders 153

Data Sources 154

Time Series 155

Variable Weights 156

Filters 156

Page Items 157

Page Item Options 159

Tables 159

Graphs 161

Shape 162

Text 163

Page Options 164

Report Options 165

Responses 166

Recorded Responses 167

Response Table 168

Advanced Options 169

Import Reponses 169

Responses in Progress 170

Download Data 172

Cross Tabulation 173

Cross Tab Table Options 174

Cross Tabulation Statistics 177

Appendix A: Question Types 179

Changing the Question Type 180

Multiple Choice 180

Matrix Table 181

Text Entry 183

Text / Graphic 184

Constant Sum 184

Slider 185

Sliding Scale 186

Rank Order 186

Pick, Group and Rank 187

Side-By-Side 188

Drill Down 189

Heat Map 190

Hot Spot 191

Gap Analysis 192

File Upload 193

Timing 193

Meta Info 195

Appendix B: Polls 197

Create a New Poll 199

Edit the Look and Feel 199

Delete a Poll 200

Appendix C: Classic Reporting 201

View Reports 202

Graphs 203

Tables 204

Notes 205

Filters 206

Report Options 208

Export Report 212

Style Editor 212

Introduction

QUALTRICS SURVEY RESEARCH SUITE

Welcome to the Complete Research Suite guide book! Our goal at Qualtrics is to make your life easier. We have provided you with a robust survey tool that simplifies your research ventures, and as a cherry on top, we would like to impart to you the wisdom of our Qualtrics University experts.

We know you're busy. You have important data to collect! You don't have months to spend on learning a new software tool. We've got you covered. Our objective is to provide you with a quick reference you can easily search to find answers to your pressing Qualtrics questions.

Of course, if you desire to become a real Qualtrics expert, this book will provide you with all the in-depth information you need to achieve mastery. You will find all the information you need to get started in the Research Suite, laid out in step-by-step detail. As you become more familiar with the tool, you can use this guide to accomplish your more advanced research objectives.

FIRST STEP! SIGN UP WITH QUALTRICS

Before getting started, you will need a Qualtrics account. There are several ways to get an account with Qualtrics:

- If you purchased an individual license, you will be given account information by your account representative. If you had a trial account at time of purchase, your account rep will automatically upgrade it for you.

- If you are a university student and your school has a Qualtrics license, you can contact your brand administrator about setting up an account through your university login page.

- If you do not currently have a license and do not belong to an organization with a license, you will need to set up a Qualtrics Trial account.

Getting a trial account is easy. Just go to www.Qualtrics.com and click the Free Account button. Click the What's Included link to see everything you get with the trial.

Chapter 1

Create and Manage Surveys

The first steps for creating a survey are critical. This chapter explains how to create, copy and even collaborate on a survey.

AFTER READING THIS CHAPTER, YOU WILL KNOW HOW TO:

- Create your first survey
- Use the *My Surveys* tasks
- Organize surveys in folders
- Use the Collaborate feature to share surveys

If you have successfully logged in to your Qualtrics account, then you are ready to create a survey. There are several options for creating a new survey, and we will help you become familiar with them in this chapter. This is the first step you will need to take as you start the survey building process.

In addition to teaching about survey creation, this chapter will go over the tools available to you in the My Surveys tab when accessing and organizing your surveys. This includes the option to sort your surveys by header and add your surveys to folders.

Creating Your First Survey

When you log in to the Qualtrics Research Suite, you will arrive in the *My Surveys* tab. If you have not yet created any surveys, you will be prompted to create a survey. To proceed, select "Click here to create your first survey." You will then be taken to the *Create Survey* tab. Alternatively, click directly on the *Create Survey* tab to see all of your survey creation options (Figure 1-1).

If you already have surveys in your account, you will see all of them listed in the *My Surveys* tab along with any surveys that have been shared with you and the task icons available associated with each survey.

Figure 1-1 Click to create first survey.

The Create Survey Tab

Once in the *Create Survey* tab, you will see that there are three main options for creating your survey: Quick Survey Builder, Create from Copy, and Survey Library. Each option, once selected, will take you into the *Edit Survey* tab where you can begin building and editing your survey.

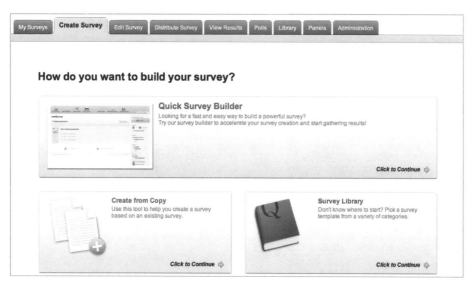

Why start with the Quick Survey Builder? Because you don't want to reinvent the wheel! Create from Copy, and Survey Library options allow you to start from a tried and true survey and make adjustments where needed.

Figure 1-2 Click to create first survey.

The **Quick Survey Builder** is called "quick" because it allows you to build a survey instantly within the Qualtrics tool. When you select this option, your survey is brought in completely blank and you can add new questions manually.

If you would like to start with a pre-existing survey, select **Create from Copy**. This is a good option if you need to build a survey similar to another survey you have in your account and just need to make a few tweaks.

Finally, there is the **Survey Library** option. This option is similar to the Create from Copy option described above, but it lets you copy from your Survey Library, a Group Library, or the Qualtrics Survey Library. Qualtrics has a whole list of already built surveys in the Qualtrics library that can be used as templates when you are just starting out. Feel free to browse them and get ideas.

QUICK SURVEY BUILDER

Clicking this option will display the Create a New Survey window (Figure 1-3).

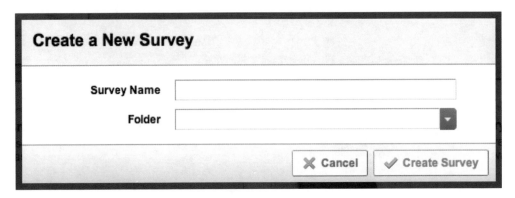

Figure 1-3 *The Create a New Survey dialog after clicking the Quick Survey Builder button.*

Since you are starting from scratch, you are asked for a survey name. You may choose to specify a folder. Once you click the **Create Survey** button, you are immediately taken to the *Edit Survey* tab so you can get to work.

CREATE FROM COPY

Clicking this option will display the Create from Copy window (Figure 1-4).

Figure 1-4 *The Create from Copy dialog window.*

You are asked which survey you would like to copy, what you would like to name it, and which folder you want to put it in. You can also copy a survey by going to the *My Surveys* tab and clicking the **Copy** button next to the survey you want to copy. You will be given a similar window to specify the survey name and folder.

SURVEY LIBRARY

Clicking this option will display the Create from Survey Library window (Figure 1-5).

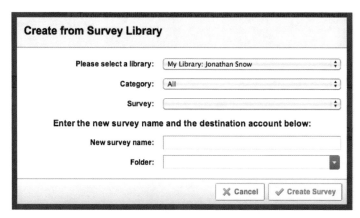

Create from Survey Library

Please select a library: | My Library: Jonathan Snow
Category: | All
Survey: |

Enter the new survey name and the destination account below:

New survey name: |
Folder: |

X Cancel   ✓ Create Survey

Figure 1-5 The Create from Survey Library dialog window.

This allows you to copy a survey from your own survey library, or copy one from the group library of a group you belong to (including the Qualtrics survey library). Simply specify which library you want to pull the survey from and use the navigation to select the survey. From there you can name the survey and place it in a folder.

Don't forget the Qualtrics Library! It contains a variety of different surveys and questions that you are welcome to copy and use.

Navigating the My Surveys Tab

Once you have created surveys in your account, you will see the My Surveys tab as a homepage where you can see the list of all your surveys and access useful tools for each of them. These tools can be found under the Tasks column.

TASK ICONS

In Figure 1-6 you can see that there is a list of Tasks on the right-hand side of each survey listed. Use these icons for quick access to the main areas of the Qualtrics survey tool. Each task correlates to the survey it is next to on the table.

Figure 1-6 *Task Icons.*

You can use the Task Icons (Figure 1-7) to jump directly to a specific task or location within the Research Suite. These icons provide one-click access to commonly used areas and features.

Figure 1-7 *A close-up of the Task Icons.*

Task Icons take you directly to the area of the tool you want with the right survey selected. Save one or two clicks in getting where you want to be.

These task icons carry out the following actions:

EDIT: Jumps to the *Edit Survey* tab of the specific survey selected.

RESULTS: Jumps to the *View Results* tab of the specific survey selected.

SEND: Jumps to the *Distribute Survey* tab of the specific survey selected.

VIEW: Opens the preview URL of the survey for testing purposes. Functions the same as the *Preview Survey* link found on the *Edit Survey* and *Distribute Survey* tabs.

COLLABORATE: Enables you to give permissions to and share a survey with another Qualtrics user so they can view, edit, distribute, and analyze data in your survey. If there isn't an existing user account for the person you want to collaborate with, then the tool will send an email and create a trial user account for them. You can read more about collaboration later on in the chapter.

COPY: Enables you to copy a survey, and even send a copy to another user account. When a copy is made, it becomes a completely separate survey with its own survey link. Survey data is **not** copied along with the survey.

TRANSLATE: Jumps to the Translate Survey feature in the *Edit Survey* tab.

DELETE: Displays a dialog box to confirm deletion, as all data is deleted with the survey. First, download a copy of your data and a copy of your survey. Use the Qualtrics Survey Format, or .qsf, for downloading your survey. A survey stored in .qsf format can be uploaded and reinstalled only into Qualtrics.

COLLABORATION

One of the most useful buttons available in the task menu is the **Collaborate** button. When clicked, it opens a window where you can choose to share your survey with another person or group.

Collaborate

Collaboration is a great way to get someone's feedback on a survey before you distribute it. Collaborators can be given permission to make edits, distribute, and even view and analyze the results of shared surveys. Don't worry, you control their access. They only have permission to perform the tasks that you specify.

To collaborate, first click the **Collaborate** task icon and enter the individual's username or email address into the text box at the top (see Figure1-8). All matches will be displayed as you type and you can select the correct one. You also have the option of clicking the **User and Group Address Book** link to the right. This gives you a list of users in your organization to select instead of typing in the username.

Figure 1-8 Add a user to share the survey within the Collaborate dialog window.

Once you've found your user, click the **Add** button. The user will then show up in the collaborate table and you will be able to specify what the user can access (Figure 1-9). In the Edit and View Results sections, you can allow all permissions by selecting the main checkbox, or be more specific by clicking the **Details** link.

ALERT: You can't give permission for the user to do anything that your personal user account doesn't give you permission to do.

When setting up the permissions you will see that there are five categories:

EDIT: Allows collaborator to Edit survey.

VIEW RESULTS: Allows collaborator to view survey results.

ACTIVATE/DEACTIVATE: Allows collaborator to activate or deactivate the survey for you.

COPY: Allows collaborator to make a copy of the survey to place and use in their own account.

DISTRIBUTE: Allows collaborator to use the Distribute Survey options

See Tables 1-1 and 1-2 for more details about the specific collaboration permission.

Most users will have the ability to share *within* their organization, but not all users will have the ability to share *outside* their organization. In fact, this is a feature mostly used in the academic world where research is shared between universities. The corporate world typically does not use this feature in an effort to keep sensitive research secure.

If you try to share a survey with someone who does not already have an account, you will be prompted to send an email to them that contains a link that, when clicked on, automatically creates a trial account for them. This allows them to collaborate with you through the trial account.

Figure 1-10 Send an email for a trial account if the person you are sharing with does not have a user account (limited to academic accounts).

Table 1-1 *Q-Reference: Edit Permission Details.*

EDIT SURVEYS*	Collaborator can use the *Edit Survey* tab and make changes to your survey.
SET SURVEY OPTIONS	Allows collaborator to use the Survey Options button on the *Edit Survey* tab.
DELETE SURVEY QUESTIONS	Just like it sounds, you can specify if you want to allow your collaborator to delete questions.
USE SKIP LOGIC	Specify whether or not the person can set skip logic within the survey.
USE QUOTAS	Choose whether or not the person can set quotas on the survey.
TRANSLATE SURVEYS	Decide whether you want to allow the person to view, add, and edit translations for the survey.

CREATE RESPONSE SETS	Pick whether or not you allow the option to create Response Sets in the Survey Options window.
EDIT SURVEY FLOW	Control whether the collaborator can work with branch logic, end of survey elements, randomizers, and other elements within the Survey Flow.
USE CONJOINT	Give permission to access the self-explicated conjoint tool under Advanced Options on the *Edit Survey* tab.
COPY SURVEY QUESTIONS	Give the ability to copy questions in the survey using the Copy Question button in the blue column to the right of each question.
EDIT SURVEY QUESTIONS	Provide the ability to edit or remove the questions already in the survey, as well as add new questions.
USE BLOCKS	Give the ability to create new question blocks within the *Edit Survey* tab.
USE TRIGGERS	Give the ability to use Email and Panel Triggers, under Advanced Options on the *Edit Survey* tab.

If you don't give access to the Edit Surveys permission, all other permissions are inaccessible.

Table 1-2 *Q-Reference: View Results Permissions Details.*

EDIT SURVEY RESULTS	Allow the collaborator to access data and be able to delete or import data on the Responses page on the View Results tab.
USE CROSS TABS	Decide whether the collaborator can build and work with Cross Tabulations on the *View Results* tab.
USE SUBGROUP ANALYSIS	Allows the collaborator to set up subgroups within reports.
VIEW SURVEY RESULTS*	Allows the collaborator to access the *View Results* tab. If unchecked, the collaborator cannot access the *View Results* tab.
VIEW RESPONSE ID	Decide whether the collaborator can view the Response ID column on the Responses page and in the files downloaded from the Download Data page.

If you don't give access to the View Survey Results permission, all other permissions are inaccessible.

Show More Data

In the right-hand corner of the *My Surveys* tab is the **Show More Data** drop-down button (see Figure 1-15). This option allows you to display or not display certain columns in the survey table. Creation Date and Modified Date are not displayed by default, but you can choose to display them.

Task Icons option in the drop-down menu allows you to select the Task icons to display in the Tasks column. Each Task icon, except for Survey Copy and Survey Delete, is accessible in other places in the Survey Research Suite. Changed settings will be remembered the next time you log in.

Figure 1-11 *Specify what should be displayed.*

In the gray navigation bar at the top of the *My Surveys* tab (Figure 1-12), you have more icons that will take you to other tabs within the tool, like Create Survey, Distribute Survey, and View Results. These icons can help you quickly navigate the tool.

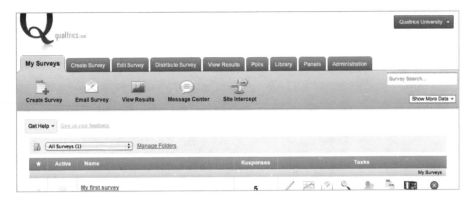

Figure 1-12 *Jump to a corresponding tab from the My Surveys tab by clicking an icon in the navigation bar.*

Organizing More Surveys

As you create more and more surveys, it may get difficult for you to find the survey you need. You're in luck! Within the
My Surveys tab there are several tools for organizing your surveys. Become familiar with these tools so you will have a clean account that is easy to navigate.

SORT BY HEADING

Each column header across the top of the survey table can be clicked. When the header is clicked, the corresponding column is sorted alphabetically, by number of responses, by date created or by date modified.

You can also star a survey (similar to flagging an email), and sort for the starred or un-starred surveys. Sorting by starred surveys will bring all of the starred surveys to the top of the list. The same goes for the active and inactive surveys. If you sort by Creation Date and Modified Date, the most recently dated surveys are brought to the top.

Figure 1-13 *Column Headers.*

FOLDERS

If you are a folder lover, you can create folders to group your surveys. At the top of the survey table is a **Manage Folders** link that expands to a folders view (see Figure 1-14).

To Manage Folders, you can do the following:
1. Click **Add Folder** to create a new folder, and **Delete Folder** to remove a selected folder.
2. Drag and drop any of your surveys on a folder to place them into that folder.
3. When you are finished making changes, click **Close**.

Folders are all about organization. Use folders to group surveys by similarity, date, or project.

Figure 1-14 *The folder management view.*

Once you have organized your surveys into folders, you can close the folder manager and go back to the survey table. Select which folder of surveys you want to look at by clicking on the drop-down menu to the left of the **Manage Folders** link.

You may assign a survey to a folder when creating it. The *Edit Survey* tab also allows you to add a survey to a folder or change which folder it is in. To do this, click on the survey name at the top of your survey while in the *Edit Survey* tab.

SEARCH

The search bar is convenient when you would like to find a survey fast. It is located near the top right of the page and allows you to search for a survey in your list of surveys by typing in the name. Your survey list will filter with matches
according to what you type.

Qualtrics searches within the folder you currently have selected.

RENAMING SURVEYS

If you have created a survey but would like to change the name, you can do so in the *Edit Survey* tab. When you click on the survey in the *My Surveys* tab, you will be taken to the *Edit Survey* tab. The survey name will show at the top of the survey. To change it, click directly on the survey name and start typing in the new name. You can change the name, as well as the folder it is in.

Research Suite Helps

As you navigate through the Research Suite, you will notice that there are many powerful tools accessible to you across every page. Feel free to use these tools as you work through your research process.

The **Current Survey Drop-Down Menu** is a convenient feature found on every page of the Suite. You can be working in one survey on the Edit Survey page and quickly change to another survey using the drop-down menu. When you go to the *Library* and *Panels* tabs, this drop-down changes to show the current library you are in or the current panel library.

The **Get Help** button is also available on each page. This button directs you to the Qualtrics University where you can
 find the following helpful tools:

- Online trainings
- Qualtrics University online documentation: www.qualtrics.com/university
- Contact information for Qualtrics: 800–340–9194, support@qualtrics.com

Please note that many of the features within the tool are permission based. While all permissions will be described here, you may not have access to a particular feature. If access is missing, please communicate with your in-house Qualtrics Administrator or contact the your Qualtrics Account Manager to gain more access.

Qualtrics University contains tons of videos, helps, and trainings. Get help when you need it.

Chapter 2

Your Account Libraries

Don't duplicate your efforts. Qualtrics saves your questions, surveys, graphics, messages and more in libraries so you can easily paste them into other places as needed.

AFTER READING THIS CHAPTER, YOU WILL KNOW HOW TO:

- Access your libraries
- Store content in your libraries
- Organize your libraries
- Share content from your libraries

Your account libraries are a great resource that you will use constantly. As you work in the tool, you will use your libraries to store graphics, organize your messages, access survey questions and much more. The Libraries are like your office file cabinets, where you can keep your important items organized. In this chapter we will teach you how to properly store items in your libraries and access them as you build and distribute your surveys.

Navigate Your Libraries

Your libraries are broken up into multiple categories: Survey Library, Questions Library, Graphics Library, Files Library, and Message Library. The Graphics Library stores graphics, the Message Library stores messages, and so on. When you enter each of these categories you will see multiple subcategories for storing your items.

Figure 2-1 *Library Tab.*

LIBRARY OVERVIEW

The Library Overview section (Figure 2-2) provides the basic information on each category in your library. You can see a clear layout of all of the categories, as well as the total number of items in each category. Each section is linked, so you can click on a category and jump directly from the Library Overview page to the individual category.

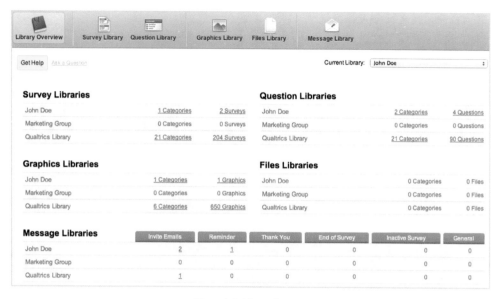

Figure 2-2 *Library Overview.*

 **SURVEY LIBRARY**

The Survey Library is where you can keep copies of surveys that you would like to reference later. While you can always make copies of your existing surveys, it's a great resource to have a library of survey templates for you and other colleagues to reference when building new surveys.

Personal, Group, and Qualtrics libraries store surveys for personal and group-wide use.

To copy a survey to a Survey Library:
1. Go to the *Library* tab and click on the **Survey Library** icon to enter the Survey Library.
2. Click the green **Copy a Survey to This Library** button.
3. In the Source Survey menu, select the survey to copy.
4. If needed, specify a category to put the survey into. This is optional. If you don't select a category, the survey will be placed into the predefined "Unassigned" category.
   - To create a new category, type it into the text field.
   - To select an existing category, click the blue arrow.
5. Under Survey Name, enter a name for the survey. It will automatically populate with the name of the survey selected.
6. Click **Copy**.

Q-TIP

You can copy a survey to a library from the *My Surveys* tab as well. Click the **Copy** button next to a survey, then under the **Copy to** menu, select **Library**.

QUESTION LIBRARY

Using the question library to store frequently used questions and layouts will speed up your survey building process.

The Question Library (Figure 2-3) is where you can keep copies of specific questions you might want to reference later on. You can copy questions into the library from existing surveys in your account. This is great when you want to have a library of question templates for you and other colleagues to reference when building a new survey.

Figure 2-3 *Question Library.*

The **Copy Items From** button at the bottom of each block in the Edit Survey tab will allow you to insert questions from your Question Library as you build your surveys.

To add a question to a Question Library:
1. Go to the *Library* tab and click on the **Question Library** icon to enter the Question Library.
2. Click the green **Copy a Question to This Library** button.
3. In the Source Survey menu, select the survey to copy.
4. In the Source Question menu, select the question to copy.
5. Under **Category**, specify a category to put the survey into. This is optional. If you don't select a category, the survey will be placed into the predefined "Unassigned" category.
   - To create a new category, type it into the text field.
   - To select an existing category, click the blue arrow.
6. Under **Description**, enter a name for the question. It will automatically populate with the name of the question selected under Source Question.
7. Click **Copy**.

GRAPHICS LIBRARY

Any images you add to the tool, whether in a question or in a message, are placed in your Graphics Library.

The Graphics Library (Figure 2-4) is where your images are stored. All images you put into your question text, answer choice text, or email messages are stored here.

When you enter the Rich Content Editor from a question, answer choice, or message, you can click on the Insert Image icon to insert an image from your graphics library. A box containing your graphics library will appear and you can choose one of your already-uploaded graphics or click **Upload a New Graphic**.

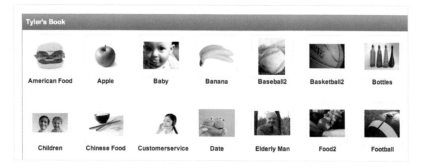

Figure 2-4 Sample Graphics Library.

You can also add graphics to your Graphics Library directly from the Library Tab.

To Upload a New Graphic while in the *Library* tab:
1. Click into the Graphics Library from the *Library* tab.
2. Click the green **Upload a New Graphic** button.
3. At this point you can select a graphic from your computer by selecting **Browse** or **Choose File**, or you can click the **Use a graphic from the web** option to paste the URL of the image you found on the internet.
4. Provide a Category. This is optional. If you choose not to specify a category, the image will be placed under the "Unassigned" category.
5. Specify a Description or name for the image. The tool will automatically grab the file name of the image.
6. If you uploaded an image from your computer, you will be able to specify a width and height to change the size of the image. The ability to modify size is not available if using the Use a graphic from the web option.
7. Click **Save**. If you are on the *Edit Survey* tab using the Rich Content Editor, clicking Save will automatically place the image into the question or answer choice text.

Make sure you have permission to use the images you upload into your library and display in your surveys.

FILES LIBRARY

The Files Library is where you will store all files that don't fall under the Graphics category. There are several situations where you will need to use your Files Library. For example, if you are attaching a file to a question in your survey so that your respondents can download it, you will store that file in your Files Library.

Store files for your respondent to view or download. Use for any file that is not a graphic image.

To Upload a New File:
1. Click into the Files Library from the Library tab then click the **Upload a New File** button.
2. Click **Browse** or **Choose File** to find the file on your computer.

3. Assign the file to a Category. This is optional. If you choose not to specify a category, the file will be placed under the "Unassigned" category.
4. Provide a Description or name for the file. By default the file will be assigned the name you gave it when you saved it on your computer.
5. Click **Save** when ready.

MESSAGE LIBRARY

The Message Library (Figure 2-5) is where all messages you use in the Research Suite are stored (survey invitation, reminder, thank you, etc.). In the Message Library you can find and edit any existing messages, as well as create new messages as needed.

Figure 2-5 *Example Message Library.*

To create a new message while in the Library tab:
1. On the Message Library page, click the **Create a New Message** button.
2. Choose a Category for your message. Categories determine where in the tool the message is available. The message library doesn't allow you to create your own category. The following categories are available: Invite Email, Reminder Email, Thank You Email, End of Survey Messages, Inactive Survey Messages, Validation Messages, General Messages, and Look and Feel Messages.

There are many times you will need to insert or create a message while you are working within the tool. When you email your survey out, for instance, or choose to change the End of Survey message, you will be prompted to choose a message or create a new one. At these times you will be able to access to your library messages through a drop-down or choose to create a new message. Any new message you create while working in the tool will be saved to the message library.

Summary

There are five subsections to your account library: Survey Library, Question Library, Graphics Library, File Library, and Message Library. Each of these libraries can be accessed within the Library tab, but they are also available throughout the tool whenever you need them. When you are in the Rich Content Editor, for example, you can select to insert a graphic and your Graphics Library will pop-up. This also applies any time you need to use a message or insert a file.

From the Library tab you can also access survey and question templates provided by Qualtrics. As you read over the next few chapters and start to build your surveys, use these templates to learn about the capacity of the tool and save time.

Chapter 3

Edit Your Survey

Qualtrics has thousands of options for you in editing your survey.
This is the first chapter that seeks to explain them all in detail.

AFTER READING THIS CHAPTER, YOU WILL KNOW HOW TO:

- Build a survey from scratch
- Edit survey questions
- Edit answer choices
- Change the appearance of your surveys
- Enable important settings in Survey Options

You will likely spend much of your questionnaire development time in the *Edit Survey* tab, so this chapter is the meat and potatoes of the book. Take some time to become familiar with the basic breakdown of how to use the *Edit Survey* tab and watch your survey building horizons widen.

In this chapter, we will first introduce how to add questions and basic elements to your survey, then examine general survey level options. Finally, we discuss how to check spelling in your survey, preview the survey and print the survey.

Once you have an idea of how to build your survey, feel free to read over the appendix at the end of this book for a detailed explanation of all question types and how to use them.

Add and Position Questions

When you click the Quick Survey Builder option and create a new survey, you are given a blank template, which is actually your Default Question Block. It is within the question block that questions are *added and edited.*

⊕ ADDING QUESTIONS WITH THE GREEN "+" BUTTONS

The easiest way to insert a question between existing questions!

Questions can be inserted after any existing question, page break, or at the bottom of a question block. Just click one of three green "+" buttons. One is found at the bottom of a question block (Create New Item). The other two are found by hovering your mouse over any question or page break – they will display at the top right and bottom right corners.

Figure 3-1 Plus buttons for adding questions to a survey.

⊙ COPY QUESTIONS FROM...

You can also pull questions from other surveys or libraries by clicking the purple **Copy Item From...** button. This allows you to select questions from other surveys in your account, or from the Survey and Question Libraries you have access to.

After clicking **Copy Item From**, you will click to drill-down to a more specific category or item until you find the desired questions. Once you see the question, hover your mouse over the question text on the left to see a preview. Click all of the questions you want to add. You can add as many as you want at one time, then click the blue **Add** button at the bottom of the window.

Copy over that awesome question you created in another survey.

Q - T I P

- Click the gray question block header in the list of questions on the left to select every question within that block at once.
- Just click a question again if you want to deselect it.
- When no questions are selected, the blue **Add** button allows you to "Import Entire Survey", which is all the questions in the list on the left.

▥ COPY QUESTION

You can add a question or group of questions to your survey by copying existing question in your survey. Do this by clicking on the question you would like to copy (the question will turn blue) and then clicking on the **Copy Question** link to the bottom right of the question in the blue column. To copy a group of questions, you can either select them by checking each checkbox near the top left of each question, or by clicking on a question and using Ctrl+click (on Macs: Cmd+click) to select additional questions individually.

You can also use Shift+click to select a large amount of questions all at once. To do this click on the first question in the list, hold down Shift then click on the last question in the list of questions you would like to copy. To the right you will have a menu of options that can be used when multiple questions are selected. Click the **Copy** button and you will copy all of the questions into your survey. These copied questions will show up below the original questions in the survey.

⊟ MOVE QUESTION

The Move Question option allows you to move your questions to a different location in the survey. When you select **Move Question**, the question you have selected turns into a light blue block that follows your mouse until you find where you want to place it.

Question in the wrong spot? Just move it to the right one.

To use Move Question:
    1. Click the question you want to move.
    2. Click **Move Question** (located at the bottom of the blue bar on the far right).

Figure 3-2 Move Question.

    3. Move your mouse to the place in the survey where you want the question to be. The light blue
       block will follow your mouse wherever you scroll.
    4. Click in the survey where you would like the question to be placed.

Q-TIP

- To move your question a short distance, hover over the question and click the up/down arrows
  that appear directly to the left of the question.
- Move multiple questions at a time by selecting multiple questions (Shift+click or Ctrl/Cmd+click,
  or click the checkboxes), then click the **Move** button to the right. Then follow steps 3 and 4 above.

Figure 3-3 Move multiple questions.

PREVIEW QUESTION

Clicking Preview Question is the equivalent to clicking Preview Survey at the top of the page, but just for
an individual question. It's a great way to see how your question will look within the selected Look and Feel
without having to click through the survey to get to it.

To use Preview Question:
1. Click the question you want to preview.
2. Click **Preview Question**. A small browser window will open, showing the question.

- Preview the entire survey by clicking **Preview Survey** at the very top of the *Edit Survey* tab. This button is also available on the *Distribute Survey* tab, as well as the *My Surveys* tab, next to each survey (the "View" button).
- Preview an entire question block by clicking **Block Options** and selecting **View Block**.

ADD A PAGE BREAK

Add Page Break allows you to break up a block of questions into separate pages. This is similar to inserting a break into a Word document. It's great to use this option when you have a lengthy block of questions. It allows you to keep your survey in screen-sized chunks so that the participant does not become overwhelmed by having to scroll through a long screen of questions.

Too many questions on a page can reduce response quality. You might also consider using Timing questions, which report page response time.

To use Add Page Break:
1. Click the question you want the break to appear after.
2. Click **Add Page Break** (located at the bottom of the blue bar on the far right).

Figure 3-4 *Add a page break.*

If you want a set number of questions per page throughout a survey, use the Questions Per Page option found under Look and Feel on the *Edit Survey* tab.

Edit Questions

SELECTING A QUESTION TYPE

When you insert a question into a survey, the default question type is multiple choice. You can change the question type by selecting the question (it turns blue), then clicking the green **Change Item Type** button (Figure 3-5) to the right of the question in the blue column. When a question type is selected, the options in the question menu bar to the right adjust according to the question type you have selected. A detailed description of each Question Type and their accompanying options is given in the appendix following this chapter (Appendix A).

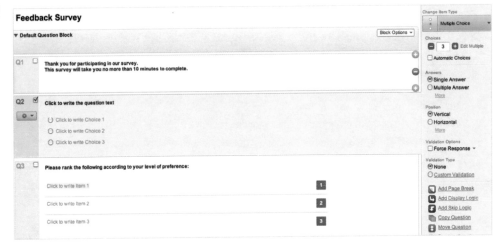

Figure 3-5 Select a question type.

ALERT: If you've already begun collecting responses, changing your question type could result in the loss of collected data.

EDITING TEXT

To edit question or answer choice text, click directly on the question text and answer choice text to write in what you would like it to say.

To customize the question text using HTML, click on the question and then click on the **HTML View** button above the question text field. The answer choice fields can receive HTML directly. If HTML isn't your skill, the Rich Content Editor is also available, providing a toolbar of options for text formatting.

To use the **Rich Content Editor** when editing question text, click the **Rich Content Editor** tab near the top left corner of the question text window.

When you are done using the Rich Content Editor, click the gray space outside of the Rich Content Editor window and the changes will automatically be saved.

Figure 3-6 Rich Content Editor menu.

When the Rich Content Editor is opened, there are buttons at the top that all serve a specific function:
- {a} **Pipe in tex**t from a question, panel, or embedded data field (first icon in the top row).
- **Insert images** into a survey or message from your graphics library. You can upload a graphic from this view as well.
- **Attach or link to files** for respondents to download from surveys or messages.
- **Insert media into your survey**, such as video or audio clips from a URL (film strip icon). You can also use the links from your Files Library and have Qualtrics host the media files.
- **Insert special characters** that you can't find on your keyboard.
- **Insert a table** in which you can then insert content.
- **Hyperlink a word or phrase** (chain link icon), or remove a hyperlink (broken chain link icon).
- **Undo/Redo changes**.
- **Align text** left, center, right, and block justify.
- **Increase/decrease indent** of text and numbering/bullet lists.
- **Insert Numbered and/or Bulleted Lists**.
- **Remove formatting** (eraser icon) from text you need to clean up.
- **Change font**.
- **Change text size**.
- **Format text** with options to bold, italicize, and underline.
- **Use subscripts or superscripts.**
- **Change text background color**, or highlight text.
- **Change text color**.
- **Use Source to view the HTML** of the text being used and edit as needed.

The Rich Content Editor will appear throughout the Research Suite whenever you need to draft a message or edit text. These same tools are available wherever you have access to the Rich Content Editor.

Q-TIP
- In the Edit Survey tab, the Rich Content Editor tab will not be available until you click the question text field you want to edit, so click in the text field to get started.
- Viewing **Source** in the Rich Content Editor is the same thing as viewing your question in **HTML View** for a question. If you would rather use code to edit your font, you can enter the code into Source or HTML View.

EDIT ANSWER CHOICES

Once you have inserted a question and written your question text, you will want to edit your answer choices. You can edit answer choices by clicking on them. When the choice is selected, it becomes highlighted and the text may be edited.

When editing an answer choice, a blue arrow appears to the right. Clicking the arrow provides a myriad of advanced options that will help you customize your answer choices (Figure 3-7).

The following section will give you details about each answer choice option.

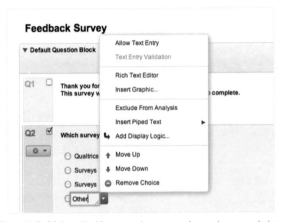

Figure 3-7 Click on the blue arrow to access advanced answer choices.

ALLOW TEXT ENTRY

Allow Text Entry places a small text field next to an answer choice. This allows respondents to enter their own information, such as their own answer choice, into the question. This is most commonly used when placing an "Other (please specify)" answer choice into the question.

To use Allow Text Entry:
1. Click to edit an answer choice.
2. Click the **blue arrow** to the right.
3. Select **Allow Text Entry**

Q-TIP

- Text entered into the text entry boxes appears as an extra column when you download your data set. The responses are displayed verbatim.
- On a multiple choice question, by default, the text entry field displays just below the choice. To make it appear directly to the side, change your multiple choice question position to Column in the question menu bar to the right. If you want just one column, then specify the number of columns as "1".

If you have selected "Allow Text Entry", then you can decide to add content validation to your text box. Text Entry Validation allows you to require that the respondent's entered text matches a particular format, such as email address, phone number, date, month, year or valid US state. Except for Force Response, these options are the same as the Content Validation options when using the Text Entry Single Line question type.

To use Text Entry Validation:
1. Click to edit an answer choice.
2. Click the **blue arrow** to the right.
3. Hover over **Text Entry Validation**.
4. Select the necessary validation option.

Force Response can be applied in addition to any content validation. Just repeat steps 1–3 above.

RICH CONTENT EDITOR FOR ANSWER CHOICES

The Rich Content Editor can also be used to edit individual answer choice text. You can edit the answer choice field by typing HTML into the answer choice text field, but the Rich Content Editor makes it much easier!

To use the Rich Content Editor for your answer choices (Figure 3-8):
1. Click the answer choice to edit it.
2. Click the **blue arrow** to the right.
3. Select **Rich Content Editor**.
4. Edit your text using the toolbar of options.
5. Click **Save** when finished.

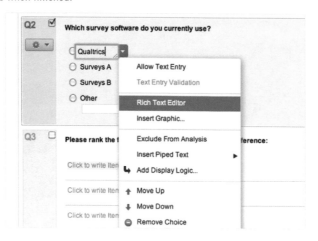

Figure 3-8 Rich Content Editor for an answer choice.

INSERT GRAPHIC

Use graphics in your survey for testing concepts or just to keep things interesting for your respondents.

This option, found in the blue arrow drop-down, makes it easy to insert a .png, .gif, or .jpg image into your answer choice field.

To use Insert Graphic:
1. Click on the answer choice you would like to edit.
2. Click the **blue arrow** to the right.
3. Select **Insert Graphic**.
4. Select an image using one of the following methods:
   a. Click the **Library** drop-down menu near the top left if grabbing an image from a group library.
   b. Click **Upload a New Graphic** if the image isn't already in your library.
      i. Click **Browse** to find the file on your computer.
      ii. Click **Use a graphic from the web** to reference an image online.

Q-TIP

- Valid file types: .png, .gif, and .jpg (.jpeg).
- Make sure you have permission to use the images you want to display in your survey.
- Images can also be inserted through the **Rich Content Editor**. Just click the **Insert Image** icon found at the top of the Rich Content Editor toolbar.

EXCLUDE FROM ANALYSIS

Exclude a particular choice from the results. A "Prefer Not to Answer" or "None of the Above" choices are common applications.

Exclude From Analysis is an off-on switch that can be selected so an answer choice and its data are not used in the tables and graphs in the reports (Figure 3-9).

To use Exclude From Analysis:
1. Click the answer choice to edit it.
2. Click the **blue arrow** to the right.
3. Select **Exclude From Analysis**.

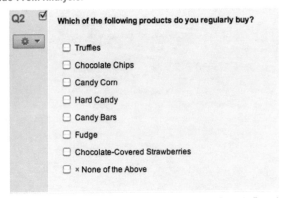

Figure 3-9 A red 'x' will appear next to an answer set with Exclude From Analysis.

- Exclude From Analysis is automatically selected when you enter None of the Above.
- An excluded choice is designated by a small red X appearing to the left of the choice.
- To turn off, just repeat steps 1–3.

INSERT PIPED TEXT

Insert Piped Text allows you to display information from other places in the survey. You can pipe text from a Survey Question, Embedded Data Field, Panel Field, Loop and Merge Field, or Quota.

To use Insert Piped Text:
1. Click the answer choice to edit it.
2. Click the **blue arrow** to the right.
3. Select **Insert Piped Text**.
4. Hover over the category you would like to pipe from: Survey Question, Embedded Data Field, Web Service, GeoIP Location, Date, Panel Field, Loop and Merge Field, or Quota.
5. Select or enter the necessary information.

It will give you a little code that is replaced with the text that gets piped. Place the code where you would like the information to show up. This can be in an answer choice or a question.

Increase respondent involvement by creating smart surveys that carry the respondent's answers or question text forward from other areas of the survey. Works with loop and merge, quotas, logic and more.

The piped text code can be formatted. The piped text will be displayed the way that it is formatted. To format the code, open the Rich Content Editor and highlight the code. Select to apply a format from the Rich Content Editor toolbar.

ADD DISPLAY LOGIC TO AN ANSWER CHOICE

In the answer choice drop-down you can also choose to add Display Logic to an answer choice. This is a great way for you to specify if a certain answer choice should be displayed conditionally.

To Add Display Logic to an answer choice:
1. Click on the answer choice you would like to display conditionally.
2. Click on the **blue arrow** to the right.
3. Select **Add Display Logic**.
4. Complete the logic statement.

You can find out more information about Display Logic and how to apply it to a whole question in Chapter 4.

Display or don't display an answer choice based on previous responses or conditions. Show their three top choices they have purchased, all as you drill down for more information.

If you need to Carry Forward choices from multiple questions, use Add Display Logic. Insert all possible choices, then set Display Logic on each choice to specify when it should be visible.

ASSIGN TO GROUP

Add a choice to a specific choice group. Choice groups will be discussed in more detail in Chapter 4: Advanced Question Options.

To add a choice to a group:
1. Click on the answer choice you would like to assign to a group.
2. Click on the blue arrow to the right.
3. Select Assign to Group.
4. Type a new group name, or select an existing group.

MOVE UP AND MOVE DOWN

Selecting **Move Up** allows you to move an answer choice up one spot.
To move a choice up one spot:
1. Click on the answer choice you would like to move up.
2. Click on the **blue arrow** to the right.
3. Select **Move Up**.

Selecting **Move Down** allows you to move an answer choice down one spot.

To move a choice down one spot:
1. Click on the answer choice you would like to move down.
2. Click on the **blue arrow** to the right.
3. Select **Move Down**.

You can insert an answer choice in between existing answer choices. Just click on the choice above where the new one should display, then press Enter on your keyboard.

REMOVE CHOICE
Remove Choice deletes the answer choice from your list of choices.

To remove an answer choice:
1. Click on the answer choice you would like to remove.
2. Click on the **blue arrow** to the right.
3. Select **Remove Choice**.

ALERT: Be careful deleting choices when you have data in your survey. Deleting an answer choice will delete the data associated with that answer choice. Deleting answer choices after activating your survey and then adding them back in can also mess up the way your choices are coded. If you do this, make sure to check your coded values before analyzing.

Q-TIP

You can also remove an answer choice by using the Backspace or Delete keys on your keyboard. Delete all the text, then press the key one more time to remove the choice. If you have data in your survey, the tool will confirm you want to delete the choice.

Reduce non-response error by requiring a certain response, content type, or just require an answer to the question.

VALIDATION

There are four main types of validation available: Force Response, Request Response, Content Type Validation (where applicable), and Custom Validation. Validation options vary with each Question type and can be viewed in the question menu bar to the right when a question is selected.

FORCE RESPONSE

Select Force Response to require respondents to answer a question before they can move on to the next page of the survey.

This option can also be applied to multiple questions at a time. Select multiple questions, either by checking the check box next to each or using your keyboard, then select **Force Response** in the group of options to the right.

Figure 3-10 Find Force Response in the question menu bar to the right.

REQUEST RESPONSE

Click the text (or arrow) for **Force Response**, then click **Request Response**. Selecting this option lets the survey taker know if they didn't answer the question, but allows them to choose whether to return to answer the question or continue. It's like a gentle reminder to answer the question.

CONTENT TYPE VALIDATION

This validation is available for text fields, like the Text Entry Single Line question type, Form Entry text fields, and even the Allow Text Entry option.

The following validation options are available:
- **EMAIL ADDRESS:** Checks if content matches the basic email address format (user@domain.top-level domain).
- **PHONE NUMBER:** Choose between United States (US), United Kingdom (UK), and Australia (AU) options.
- **US STATE:** Checks if entered text is a state name or postal code abbreviation (California or CA).
- **US ZIP CODE:** The entered text must be in the following formats: ##### or #####-####.
- **DATE:** Require the date be in the mm/dd/yyyy format, or the dd/mm/yyyy format.
- **NUMBER:** Only numeric characters are allowed.
- **TEXT ONLY (NON-NUMERIC):** Allows only regular text, no numbers or punctuation.

Q - T I P

- Content Validation is only checked after the content is entered. It does not force a response.
  - To force this information to be entered, select the Force Response option as well.
- Any entry meeting the content validation requirements will pass the Forced Response validation as well.

CUSTOM VALIDATION

Custom Validation allows you to specify certain criteria, and only allows the respondent to get past the question if they meet the criteria. You can then display a custom message to the respondent if/when they don't meet the criteria.

When you click **Custom Validation**, a special dialog window will display for setting it up.
1. Select the question you want to base the logic upon.
2. Select the choice. Most questions list the potential choices here. Text Entry fields will have you select the question again in order to move to the next drop-down.
3. Specify the criteria.
   - Most questions will show Selected, Not Selected, Displayed, and Not Displayed as the available options.
   - Text Entry field options are: Equal/Not Equal to, Greater/Less Than, Greater/Less Than or Equal to, Empty/Not Empty, Contains/Does Not Contain, Matches Regex, and Displayed/Not Displayed. Then specify what value the entered text should be compared against.
4. Choose an error message to display on failure.
   - Load a saved Message or choose from System Defaults.
9. Load a saved Message, choose from System Defaults, or create a new one (click **Load a Saved Message**, select your library, then click **New Message**...).

- The green plus button allows you to edit the text and specify a new error category, if needed.
5. Click **Save**.

 Q - T I P

Custom Validation does not have to be based off the question being edited, but can be based off any other question in the survey.

Look and Feel

So far, we have gone over how to put questions in your survey and edit them. When you have the building blocks in place for your survey, you will want to format and personalize the appearance. This is what the Look and Feel is for.

You can access the Look and Feel through the icon located on the far left-hand side of the navigation bar in the *Edit Survey* tab (Figure 3-11). There are five aspects to the Look and Feel section:

- Skins   • Fonts   • Advanced (Header, Footer, Cascading Style Sheets)
- General   • Colors

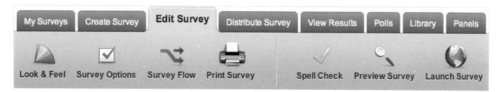

Figure 3-11 *The Edit Survey tab with Look & Feel button.*

SKINS

A skin is a template you select for the overall appearance (background, text color, etc.) of your survey. You can change the skin in the upper left hand corner of the Look and Feel (Figure 3-12).

Figure 3-12 *Clicking this allows you to select a new skin.*

Customize the appearance of your survey by changing the Look and Feel, or skin. Most organizations will have at least one skin branded specifically for them.

To Select a **Skin**:
1. Click on the drop-down menu above the thumbnail and select the Qualtrics brand library or your own organization's library of skins.
2. Click the thumbnail itself to see the available skins within your chosen library.
3. Click on the skin of your choice.

GENERAL TAB

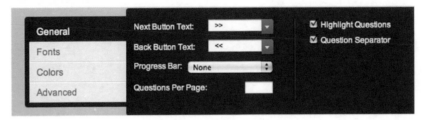

Figure 3-13 *Available options of the General tab.*

Some of the most common settings people want to change on their surveys are shown in Figure 3-13 and include:

- **NEXT/BACK BUTTON:** Change the text that appears on the button. Click the **blue arrow** to select a message or create a new one.

If altering the Back Button Text, remember to enable the Back Button option under Survey Options first.

- **PROGRESS BAR:** Want to display a progress bar in the survey? There are several options:
  - **NONE:** The default. No progress bar will display.
  - **WITH TEXT:** Displays a bar with "0%" and "100%" on either side.
  - **WITHOUT TEXT:** Displays a bar without "0%", "100%", or any other text.
  - **WITH VERBOSE TEXT:** In order to better explain to survey takers what they are looking at, this displays "Survey Completion" above the progress bar, along with "0%" and "100%" on either side.

- **QUESTIONS PER PAGE:** Type in a number to specify how many questions should display on each page. This is easier than placing page breaks everywhere, especially if you want just one question per page.

- **HIGHLIGHT QUESTIONS:** If selected, the question is highlighted when a survey taker clicks anywhere within the question. This can improve the respondent's experience by accentuating the question that is currently being answered.

- **QUESTION SEPARATOR:** Displays a line or extra space between questions (depending on the template selected).

FONTS TAB

Figure 3-14 Available options of the Fonts tab.

Here you can change the font styles and font sizes in your survey. You can select to change the font for the entire survey or specify the font styles for the Question and Choice text individually.

- **ENTIRE SURVEY:** At the top, select the font drop-down and select a font style. Then click on the Font size drop-down to choose a font size.

- **CHANGE QUESTION TEXT:** Change the font, font size, and basic formatting (bold, underline, italic) for question text across the entire survey by checking this option.

- **CHANGE CHOICE TEXT:** Change the font, font size, and basic formatting (bold, underline, italic) for choice text across entire survey by checking this option.

The Look and Feel settings will not override styles applied through the Rich Content Editor on each individual question.

COLORS TAB

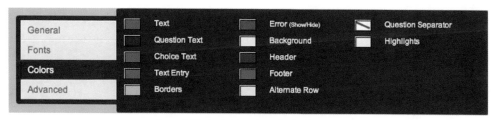

Figure 3-15 Available options in the Colors tab.

The Colors tab allows you to change the colors of the different elements in your survey. This is where you can really alter the look of your survey.

To edit your survey colors:
1. Click the **color square** or text of an element to change that color. The default skin colors are shown.

2. A color spectrum and color hex code box will appear. You can choose the color you would like to use for the element you want to alter. The vertical slider on the right can be used to alter the color palette. If you know the HTML color code you want, you can enter that into the text field at the bottom (#XXXXXX).

To **remove** edited colors:
- After altering a color, click the red "**x**" to return to the default.
- Remove all color edits by clicking the **Reset Colors** button.

ADVANCED TAB

Figure 3-16 Available options of the Advanced tab.

In the Advanced Tab you can insert and edit your survey's header and footer or further alter the look of your survey using CSS (Cascading Style Sheets).

- **EDIT:** Click the **edit** button under the header or footer to open the Rich Content Editor. In the Rich Content Editor you can insert an image or text.

- **CSS:** Cascading Style Sheets are a common way to edit the look and feel of websites. These are advanced editing options. Go to Qualtrics.com/University and search "Example Stylesheet" for a CSS example.

- **ADD CUSTOM CSS:** If you're familiar with CSS, feel free to click this button to access the CSS editor. You can use this feature to further change the look and feel of your survey template.

- **EXTERNAL CSS:** If you have a file hosted online you would like to reference, place the URL to the file here.

After changing the Look and Feel options, save your changes by clicking on the **Save** option in the bottom right-hand corner, and you will return to the main *Edit Survey* section.

☑ Survey Options

Next to the Look and Feel icon on the navigation bar is the Survey Options icon. The Survey Options page includes options for survey experience, protection, termination, and response rules This page is divided into six areas: Survey Experience, Survey Protection, Survey Termination, Inactive Surveys, Partial Completion, and Response Set (Figure 3-17).

Control the respondent experience using the many options. Display a Back Button, send a Thank You email, lock down the survey to prevent multiple submissions, and set survey activation and deactivation dates and times.

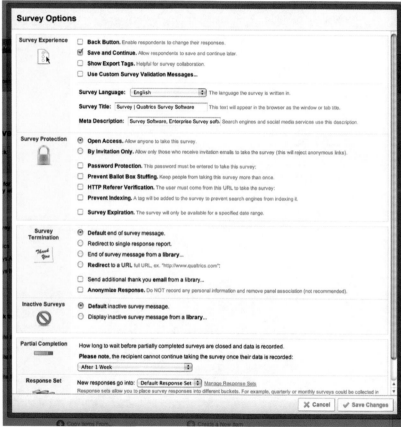

Figure 3-17 *Survey Options Window.*

The most common settings are in place as the default. Be sure to double-check the Survey Options to make sure they fit your needs before distributing your survey.

SURVEY EXPERIENCE

The Survey Experience options are mainly options that affect how the survey displays to the survey taker. Other options affect how respondents are able to Save and Continue the survey later.

- **BACK BUTTON:** The Back Button option allows respondents to go back to previous pages in the survey. This option is disabled by default.

This option can conflict with elements in the Survey Flow. If advanced elements (e.g., embedded data, branch) are in the Survey Flow between blocks, respondents will not be able to go back across those blocks.

- **SAVE AND CONTINUE:** Uses a cookie stored on the respondent's browser to keep track of how far in the survey the respondent has progressed. If the respondent exits the survey early, this option allows them to simply click the link to return to where they left off.

This is machine and browser dependent. If someone starts the survey at work and then goes home to continue from a different machine, there won't be a cookie for the tool to know where they left off and it will not start them where they left off. This option is designed for use with the Anonymous Survey Link (found in the *Distribute Survey* tab) where no tracking is included. Save and Continue is not necessary when using the Authenticator or the unique link from the survey mailer.

- **SURVEY LANGUAGE:** Choose the default language of your survey. This affects the display language of default error and end of survey messages.

If you need multiple languages for your survey, try using the Translate Survey option in the Advanced Options menu (*Edit Survey* tab).

- **SHOW EXPORT TAGS:** Specify if you want to show Export Tags to survey takers or not. Export Tags are the question numbers appearing at the top left corner of each question on the *Edit Survey* tab.

Change Export Tags by clicking on them. Once selected, you can type in a different number or change the tag to a letter. Alternatively, you can use the Auto-Number Questions option in the Advanced Options menu (far right side of the *Edit Survey* tab).

- **SURVEY TITLE:** Specify the title text that appears in the browser window/tab for your survey.

SURVEY PROTECTION

Survey Protection provides some control over how people access the survey and how frequently they can access the survey.

Control when and under what conditions your survey can be taken and re-taken.

- **OPEN ACCESS:** When this option is selected, the survey can be taken through the anonymous survey link. The survey taker does not have to click the unique link from the Email Survey page to access the survey. To limit the access, change the setting to **By Invitation Only**.

- **BY INVITATION ONLY:** This is only for use with the unique link you get from the Email Survey page. When this is enabled, the participant must click the unique link to access the survey.

- **PASSWORD PROTECTION:** This enables you to set a single password for your survey.

    If you need a unique password for each survey taker, use the Authenticator option in the Survey Flow (see Survey Flow section in Chapter 5).

- **PREVENT BALLOT-BOX STUFFING:** This keeps people from taking the survey more than once. Qualtrics uses a browser-based cookie to mark if someone took the survey. If they attempt to take the survey again, they will be kept out.

- **HTTP REFERER VERIFICATION:** This enables you to specify a URL users have to come from in order to take the survey. It is useful if your survey link is posted on a particular website (like an internal university or company page) and you want to make sure the link does not get copied and sent to others. Only those who can access the url you specify will be able to take the survey.

- **PREVENT INDEXING:** This option prevents Google, Yahoo, Bing and other search engines from being able to index your survey and present it in search results. Typically, this is only an issue for long-term studies where the survey is active for a long time.

- **THIS SURVEY DOES NOT EXPIRE:** If this option is selected, there is no set date range for when respondents are able to access the survey. If the survey is active, the link can be accessed.

- **THIS SURVEY IS VALID FROM:** This enables you to specify a date range when respondents can access the survey. Click the calendar icon or enter in the date directly (YYYY-MM-DD) to specify a date range. Those trying to access the survey before or after the specified range receive a simple message explaining it is currently unavailable.

SURVEY TERMINATION

*Use a Thank
You message
to show
appreciation
or a redirect to
drive traffic to
your website.*

The Survey Termination options are great if you want to show a custom thank you message at the end of your survey or redirect your respondent to your website when they submit their response. Here is a list of all of the options under Survey Termination and what they do:

- **DEFAULT END OF SURVEY MESSAGE:** Respondents will get this message if you have not chosen one of the other custom messages. The text displayed is, "We thank you for your time spent taking this survey. Your response has been recorded."

- **REDIRECT TO A SINGLE RESPONSE REPORT:** Redirect the respondent to a report that displays their responses. The report they see is similar to the report found under the Responses page. The respondent is given the option of exporting the report as a PDF.

An alternative approach is to customize an End of Survey element in the Survey Flow and select **Show Response Summary**, which displays a view of the survey questions with their selections in place. This can also be exported to PDF.

- **END OF SURVEY MESSAGE FROM A LIBRARY:** This allows you to create and select your own message to display to respondents.

Insert additional End of Survey elements in the Survey Flow to have multiple messages in place. Use the Branch Logic to control when each displays.

- **SEND A THANK YOU EMAIL FROM A LIBRARY:** Specify a Thank You message for the system to send out to each survey taker as their completed response comes in. This only sends to those who have completed the survey.

This only works if you email the survey to a panel on the Distribute Survey tab using the unique link (the default setting). Go to the Email History page to send a one-time Thank You email blast to all who completed the survey.

These Survey Termination options are also available when customizing an End of Survey element in the Survey Flow.

*Display a
custom message
when someone
tries to access
your survey
after you
deactivated it.*

INACTIVE SURVEYS

Under the Inactive Survey section, you can choose the message that will appear when you deactivate your survey. You can either use the default inactive survey message or create one of your own using the message library.

- Default inactive survey message: If the survey is inactive/deactivated, the default message is, "Thank you for your time, unfortunately this survey has been closed."

You can determine if your survey is active by looking at the Active column on the *My Surveys* tab. If a gray box displays, it's inactive. If it's a green checkbox, then it's active.

- Display inactive survey message from a library: Create and select your own custom message when the survey is inactive.

PARTIAL COMPLETION

Partial Completion allows you specify the amount of time your respondents have to finish the survey once they have started it. If someone starts the survey, but is unable to complete it in one sitting, the system starts counting down from their last activity. If no activity occurs within the time frame you select, their survey session is closed and whatever data has been entered is available in your reports. If they access the survey again before the time runs out, then the countdown restarts. There are many timeframes to choose from, as seen in Figure 3-18.

If someone doesn't finish their survey, what happens? How long do you wait, and do you report their data up to that point, or throw it out completely?

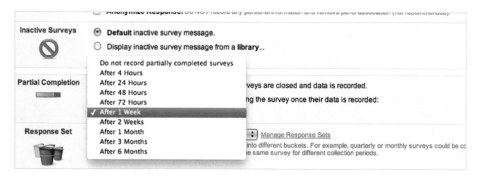

Figure 3-18 *Timeframes available under Partial Completion.*

The **Do not record partially completed surveys** option provides a week's time for the respondent to return to complete the survey. If they do not return, the survey session is closed and **their response is not stored**.

- A Survey Session is created whenever someone starts a survey. The participant's individual response is a survey session.
  - Once the survey session is closed, it cannot be reopened. As long as **Do not record partially completed surveys** is not selected you can use the **Retake Survey** and **Retake Survey as New Response** options on the Responses page. These options generate a new link that you can send to the respondent. The **Retake Survey** link will contain any data the respondent had in their previous response.
- The respondent's ability to return to the survey depends on the kind of link you are using. If you

are using a unique link sent through the mailer, the respondent can click on the link to continue taking the survey. If you are using the anonymous survey link, with **Save and Continue** enabled, the respondent can click the anonymous survey link. If they are in the same browser on the same machine they were using when they started the survey, they can see their responses up to that point and continue taking the survey.

RESPONSE SET

Response Sets allow you to place survey responses into different data collection buckets. For example, quarterly or monthly surveys could be collected in different buckets. This allows you to view results of the same survey for different data collection periods. Response Sets are added by checking on the Manage Response Sets link, where multiple Response Sets can be created. The Default Response Set is in place for all surveys. Note that data from response sets cannot be analyzed together in the Reporting tool. The data is stored in different buckets that are meant to be kept apart.

Spell Check

Qualtrics can improve your survey quality by running a spell check before going live with a survey.

Also found in the Edit Survey navigation bar is the **Spell Check** option. You can use this built-in Spell Check tool for scanning question text and answer choices (Figure 3-19). Alternate spellings are suggested for text identified as potential misspellings.

Figure 3-19 Spell Check in action.

To use Spell Check:
1. At any time during the survey building process, click **Spell Check** under the *Edit Survey* tab. The spell check window will drop-down from the top of the page.
2. If a potential misspelling is found, select the correct spelling in the Suggestions list. The Spell Check tool will automatically move to the next potentially misspelled word.

- If the correct spelling is not found, type the correct spelling into the text box and click the **Use This Spelling** button that appears to the right.
- Use the **Next Word** and **Preview Word** buttons to navigate through the list.
- Click **Next Word** to ignore the potential misspelling, or **Ignore All** to ignore all instances of that word in the survey.
- When the tool finishes checking your spelling it will say, "Finished spell checking survey..."
- Click **Done** to terminate the Spell Check tool before it is finished.

⚲ Preview Survey

There is a Preview Survey button found on the *Edit Survey* tab, but you can also preview the survey from the *Distribute Survey* tab, as well as by clicking the View button under the *My Surveys* tab. Clicking one of these buttons opens a new browser window for testing out your survey (Figure 3-20). The survey will appear exactly the way survey takers will see it, except for a white bar across the top of the page. The white bar won't be there for the actual survey takers, but it's great for you because it contains some simple preview survey tools to help you test your survey.

Yes, you can preview your survey without having to answer. It provides useful tools to aid in the testing process.

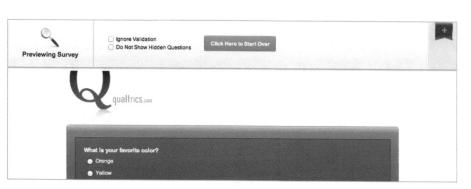

Figure 3-20 After clicking the Preview Survey button.

Preview Survey tools:
- **IGNORE VALIDATION:** If you have Force Response, Request Response, or any Content Validation or Custom Validation applied to your questions, you can check the box for Ignore Validation. This is probably the most useful of the testing tools, as you can quickly skip over the questions that would typically force you to answer.
  - This option is *not available for your survey takers*. It is only an option for you when previewing your survey.

- **DO NOT SHOW HIDDEN QUESTIONS:** Timing and Meta Info question types are automatically hidden from the survey taker's view, but they are automatically shown to you in the Preview Survey view. This is for testing purposes. You can make sure the question is in the right place and correctly taking effect. Select this option to not see these hidden questions in the preview.

- **CLICK HERE TO START OVER:** Just like it sounds, clicking this option will jump you back to the beginning of the survey. It is a great option when you would like to make changes to a specific section of your survey. You can quickly jump back to the beginning and restart testing.

- **BOOKMARK:** Click here to save your progress in the survey preview. The next time you preview the survey, you'll have the option to **Start From Bookmark** rather than having to start at the beginning.

Q-TIP

- If you click through your entire survey in Preview Survey, a response will be recorded. This response does not count toward any response quota that may be a part of your license. You can always delete these responses by going to the Responses page in the View Results tab, before collecting actual data.

Print Survey

Print directly from the browser or export the survey to Microsoft Word and then print.

Finally, we have reached the Print Survey icon in the *Edit Survey* tab. Clicking Print Survey will open a separate window containing your survey with the Look and Feel settings you have chosen. (Figure 3-21). The version of the survey in this window is more printer friendly because it places every question on one page. It will also open your browser's print dialog box.

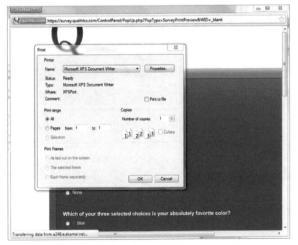

Figure 3-21 After clicking the Print Survey button.

To use Print Survey:

    1. On the *Edit Survey* tab, click the **Print Survey** button at the top of the page.

    2. In the Print dialog, adjust any settings as needed, then click **OK** to start printing.

ALERT: While the Print Survey window will contain any background images and colors, most browsers are designed not to print them. The purpose is to save you ink, since printing from the web is often done for the textual content, rather than for the images and colors. Internet Explorer 8 and older have a **Print background colors and images** option you can select. This is done by selecting **Tools**, **Internet Options** and then **Advanced**.

In many cases, especially when needing a printed survey for paper surveys, the **Export Survey to Word** is more useful than the **Print Survey** option.

Summary

In this chapter, you learned how to add questions to your survey and edit them through customizing the question text and answer choices. We went over the many Look and Feel options available to help you customize the appearance of your survey and covered the important options found in the Survey Options tab.

After reading this chapter you should have the ability to build a basic survey in the Research Suite and use the main tools in the *Edit Survey* tab. If you have more questions about question types, Appendix A goes over all of the question types available to you and will shed light on which questions you should use.

Now that you are familiar with the survey basics, read on to Chapter 4 for information on how to add complex logic to your survey as well as use the more advanced tools specific to setting up a question.

Chapter 4

Advanced Question Options

This chapter covers everything related to individual questions.

AFTER READING THIS CHAPTER, YOU WILL KNOW HOW TO:

- Use advanced logic on questions
- Access advanced question options from the Purple Gear Button, including Carry Forward Choices, Add JavaScript, and Add Default Choices
- Randomize answer choices
- Recode Values
- Check Survey Accessibility

In this chapter we continue to explore options found in the *Edit Survey* tab, but focus on the more advanced functions that you might find useful as your surveys become more complex. In the past, when paper surveys were more prevalent, survey takers would have to flip through pages of the survey to find the questions that applied to them. With the options found in this chapter, you can automate the logic in your survey, displaying questions only when they are needed.

Also gone are the days of having to manually assign values to each of your answer choices. Qualtrics automatically assigns numeric values to each choice and allows you to edit them.

This chapter is full of features that were developed to make survey building easier. Use these options to create expert surveys with very little legwork on your part.

Advanced Question Options Button

Additional functionality for a question is found by clicking the purple gear button.

Advanced Question Options are available in two locations. You may have noticed every time you click on a question, a purple gear button displays to the left of the question. Clicking the **purple gear button** opens a menu of Advanced Question Options (Figure 4-1).

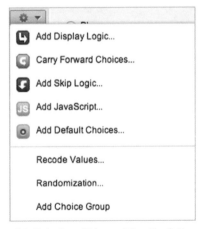

Figure 4-1 Main view of Advanced Question Options menu.

Additional options are found in the blue question menu bar to the right of the question. These options don't fall under the Advanced Question Options menu, but they are useful question-specific options to be aware of.

Some important options are also found in the Advanced Options drop-down menu in the *Edit Survey* tab. This drop-down can be found in the upper right hand corner of the screen.

ADD DISPLAY LOGIC

The **Add Display Logic** option is the first option listed under the purple gear button. Display Logic is used to display a question conditionally, based on the logic you set up in the survey. If you want to display a question only if a certain condition is met (a question answered a certain way, a particular embedded data is assigned, etc.), then you will use Display Logic. Clicking the "+" button allows you to place advanced "And If" and "Or If" statements in your logic.

You can target respondents and display questions conditionally based upon previous responses or embedded data. Display Logic is like Skip Logic, but specific to showing that particular question.

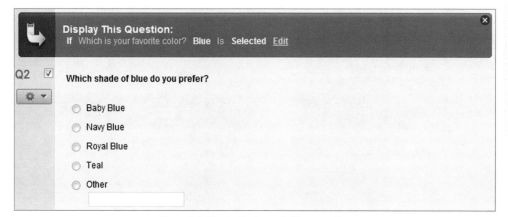

Figure 4-2 *Display Logic applied to a question.*

The Add Display Logic button is also available in the question menu bar to the right of the selected question being edited.

To set up Display Logic:
1. Select the question that you would like to display conditionally.
2. Click the **purple gear button** to the left and select **Add Display Logic**.
3. Complete the logic statement. The menus will guide you through the logic setup.
   - Logic can be based upon a question response, embedded data, quota, or panel field.
   - Add additional conditions by clicking the "+" button.
4. Click **Save** to apply the logic.

To edit existing Display Logic, click Edit on the blue Display Logic bar that appears on the question when the Display Logic is applied.

You can apply Display Logic to individual answer choices as well. Click on the answer choice to edit a choice, click the **blue arrow**, and select **Add Display Logic**.

CARRY FORWARD CHOICES

Test items most important to the respondent. Bring in selected or unselected answer choices from a previous question. It can even be used in conjunction with new choices you add to the question.

Carry Forward Choices allows you to dynamically adjust which choices are displayed to your respondents (Figure 4-3). As an example of this two-step process, the respondent would select the stores they have shopped at in the last 12 months and, where the respondent is asked to select their favorite store, only the previously selected choices would be displayed.

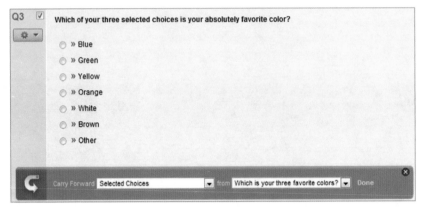

Figure 4-3 *Carry Forward Choices applied to a question.*

To set up the Carry Forward Choices option:
1. Select the question that the items will be carried into.
2. Click the **purple gear button** to the left and select **Carry Forward Choices**.
3. On the green bar that appears below the question, specify which choices are carried forward:
   - Choose to carry forward **All Choices**, **Selected Choices**, or **Unselected Choices**. Selected Choices is the most commonly selected option.
   - Select the question containing the original choices you would like to carry forward.
4. When finished, click **Done**.

To edit or delete existing Carry Forward Choices logic:
- To Edit, click **Edit** on the Carry Forward Choices bar to change your logic. From here, just re-specify the choices.
- To Delete, click the **X** at the top right of the green Carry Forward Choices bar.

- With Carry Forward Choices, you can have pre-existing answer choices in the question you are carrying forward to. Add them like you would normal choices (you might need to click the "+" Choices button below the Change Item Type menu). The pre-existing answer choices will show in the question as well as any carried forward choices.

- Carry Forward Choices can only pull from one question at a time. If you need Carry Forward Choices from multiple questions, you're better off not using Carry Forward Choices. Instead, create a new question that shows all the potential choices from all the different questions, then add Display Logic to each individual choice, specifying when each individual choice should be displayed.

ADD SKIP LOGIC

Skip Logic is a simple way to skip or jump over multiple questions. Unlike Display Logic, Skip Logic is added to the question you want to skip from (Figure 4-4). Multiple lines of logic can be put in place, but they are not linked together. Instead, the logic is evaluated from the top to the bottom of the logic condition list. Whichever logic condition is met first is the one that is applied.

Similar to Display Logic, except you can actually have the survey conditionally skip over multiple questions.

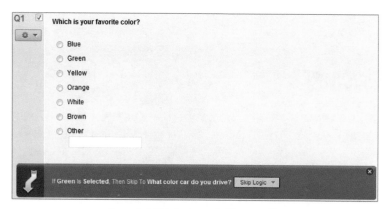

Figure 4-4 Skip Logic applied to a question.

Add Skip Logic is also available in the question menu bar to the right of the question being edited.

To use Skip Logic:
1. Select the question you would like to skip from.
2. Click the **purple gear button** to the left and select **Add Skip Logic**.
3. In the first two drop-down menus, set the condition that triggers the Skip Logic (which choice and the action — Selected, Not Selected, Displayed, or Not Displayed).
4. In the third menu, specify where to send the respondent. This can be to another question within the block, or directly to the end of the block or to the end of the survey. You cannot skip to the middle of another block.
5. When finished, click **Done**.

After you click Done, you'll notice there is a drop-down menu of options available called "Skip Logic". The options found in the drop-down are as follows:
- **EDIT SKIP LOGIC:** To edit existing Skip Logic, select this option.
- **ADVANCED OPTIONS:** Do you want to include a Quota as part of your Skip Logic? Whatever action

you have selected for the Quota will take effect (For example, End Survey will occur in place of skipping to the specified question).

- **QUOTAS:** To setup quotas for each answer choice, see Quotas under the Advanced Options drop-down menu (located at the far right of the *Edit Surveys* tab).
- **GO TO SKIP DESTINATION:** Select this option to jump down to the destination question while in the Edit Survey view. There will also be a colored arrow next to the question being skipped to.
- **REMOVE SKIP LOGIC:** Selecting this option deletes this particular line of Skip Logic.
    - If you have multiple lines of Skip Logic, you can delete them all at once by clicking the "**x**" at the top right of the Skip Logic bar.

Q - T I P

You can only use Skip Logic to jump to questions within your current question block. If you need to jump to a question in another block, you will need to either (1) use a combination of Skip Logic with Display (Skip to the end of the block, then use Display Logic to display or not display particular questions), or (2) use Branch Logic to skip over groups of questions, skipping people to the end of a block then branching people off to a block of questions if they meet the condition.

ADD JAVASCRIPT

We open the box for you. Experimental controls and other advanced features can be added by inserting javascript code.

The Qualtrics team works hard to make it so you don't ever need extra code to set up your survey. But hey, let's face it, we can't account for every unique experiment or study performed by the world's leading researchers. For that reason, Qualtrics gives you the ability to add your own code to your survey (Figure 4-5). The Add Javascript option is the fourth option under the Purple Gear button.

Figure 4-5 *Add JavaScript window.*

If you don't know what JavaScript is, you will probably need to get a good JavaScript programmer to work with you. However, we will explain how your JavaScript code can be inserted into your Qualtrics survey.

To Add JavaScript:
1. Select the question to which you would like to add JavaScript.
2. Click the **purple gear button** to the left of the question, and select **Add JavaScript**.
3. Place your cursor after the gold text that says, "/*Place Your JavaScript Below This Line*/" and press **Enter**.

4. Paste in your script (Ctrl/Cmd+v).

5. Click **Save** when done. A JavaScript icon ("JS") will now display to the left of the question.

To remove your JavaScript:

1. Click the **JS** icon to the left of the question.

2. In the editor, click the **Clear** button.

3. Click **Save**.

Q-TIP

- To preview your changes, click **Preview Survey** or **Preview Question**.
- For some useful scripts, go to **Qualtrics.com/University**, and find the Coder's Corner in the bottom left-hand corner of the page. There you will find a list of scripts for a variety of special tasks. Use any of these to experiment with the Add JavaScript option.

ALERT: The Qualtrics University team (the Support staff), is specifically trained on the survey tool, but not specifically trained in JavaScript. They are not set up to figure out bugs or issues in scripts you have written.

ADD DEFAULT CHOICES

Add Default Choices allows you to specify particular choices as pre-selected (Figure 4-6). The respondent then has the ability to leave the choice selected as is, or change it to a choice that more accurately describes their situation.

Preselect the default choice and then let respondents select a more accurate response.

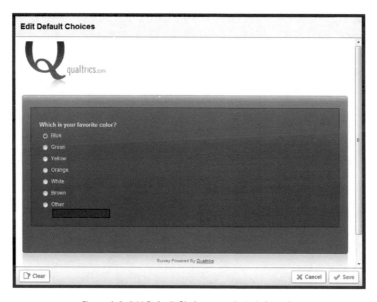

Figure 4-6 Add Default Choices preselect choices view.

To use Add Default Choices:
1. Click on the question you want to add default choices to.
2. Click the **purple gear button** to left of the question and select **Add Default Choices**.
3. In the window that opens, your question will appear and you can click the choices you want to have pre-selected.
   - With Text Entry and Constant Sum questions, you can enter the text and/or numbers you want to display.
4. Click **Save**.

RECODE VALUES

True up your reverse scaled items so they match the rest of your scale items for the analysis. This useful tool changes the numeric answer choice values.

Selecting Recode Values opens the recode wizard, and within the wizard, there are two tasks available to you: Recode Values and Variable Naming (Figure 4-7). These options allow you to change the value and assign alternate text to answer choices.

Figure 4-7 *Recode Values window.*

RECODE VALUES OPTION

Each answer choice for your question is given an answer choice value. The Qualtrics Survey Research Suite uses this value to identify the answer choice. This same value is used in the reports (basic statistics) and Download Data page exports. Recode Values allows you to change the value used for the statistics and data exports, as needed.

Recoding is often used to reverse the coding on scales, like on a Matrix-Likert question. If a scale is positive (Strongly Agree) on the left side and negative (Strongly Disagree) on the right side, then the positive scale points will have a lower value than the negative scale points. To reverse the scale or recode values, you can do the following:

1. Click the **purple gear button** to left of question, and select **Recode Values**.
2. Select the **Recode Values** checkbox.
3. Change the value in the **yellow boxes** next to each choice.

Combine answer choices in reporting by recoding answer choices to the same value (e.g., recode both as a "3"). For example, on a five point scale you might combine the top two boxes (Satisfied and Very Satisfied), as well as the bottom two boxes (Dissatisfied and Very Dissatisfied).

VARIABLE NAMING OPTION

Variable Naming allows you to assign a label for an answer choice. This is useful when wanting to shorten long answer choices or to use internal labels to represent choices. These changes are visible in reports and Download Data page exports.

To use Variable Naming:
1. Click the **purple gear button** to the left of the question, and select **Recode Values**.
2. Select the **Variable Naming** checkbox.
3. Change the label in the **pink boxes** next to each choice.

When combining answer choices (refer to Q-tip under Recode Values), assign the same name/label to the choices being combined.

Useful for avoiding any sort of response bias. Many randomization options allow you to control the choice display order to your respondents.

QUESTION EXPORT TAGS

When you click **Recode Values** for a Matrix question, you will be given the Question Export Tags option. This allows you to assign an export tag to each row of your matrix, much like the export tags of an individual question (the question numbering). This is visible as part of the data you export from the Download Data page.

To see and change Question Export Tags:
1. On a Matrix question, click the **purple gear button** to the left of the question, and select **Recode Values**.
2. Select the **Question Export Tags** checkbox.
3. In the **blue boxes** next to each choice, change the export tag.

RANDOMIZATION

Randomization gives you the option of randomizing the choices displayed in a question. This function is important in preventing question order bias. Selecting **Randomization** will open a Choice Randomization window (Figure 4–8).

While an answer choice might have a lot of text for the respondent, you can have it display a more succinct title to help you and your colleagues when looking at the data.

Figure 4-8 Randomization options for answer choices.

Once you apply Randomization to a question, a randomization icon (as seen in Figure 4-9) will appear on the left.

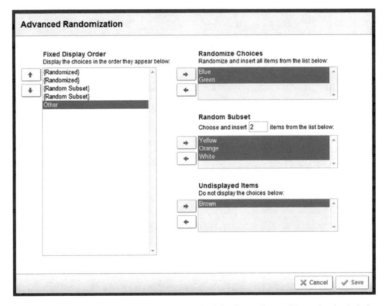

Figure 4-9 The Randomization icon displays to the left of questions with randomized choices.

There are four options in the Randomization window:

- **NO RANDOMIZATION:** The default selection. Choices are not randomized.
- **RANDOMIZE THE ORDER OF ALL CHOICES:** This automatically takes all choices and randomizes the order when displayed to the respondent.
- **PRESENT ONLY __ OF TOTAL CHOICES:** This allows you to specify a number of choices to be randomly selected and displayed (for example, 4 of 7 could be displayed).
- **ADVANCED RANDOMIZATION:** Allows for more control over the randomization options. You can even combine fixed and random display options for choice variables. By viewing the Advanced Randomization tables, you can see which choices are in a fixed position and which are randomized. Click **Set Up Advanced Randomization** to access these options:
  - **FIXED DISPLAY ORDER:** A subset (or all) choices are selected and the order of presentation is fixed.

- **RANDOMIZE CHOICES:** Randomizes order of all choices moved into this area.
- **RANDOMIZE SUBSET:** Specify a number of choices to randomly choose and display (2 of 4, 3 of 7, etc.)
- **UNDISPLAYED ITEMS:** Specify certain choices you don't want displayed at all.

To add answer choices to the different randomization option boxes:
1. Click to select the choices to randomize (Shift+click or Ctrl/Cmd+click to select multiple).
2. Click the arrow pointing to the right to pull the choices into any of the three randomization option boxes on the right.
3. Repeat steps 1 and 2 for other randomization options you want to implement (Figure 4-10).

CHOICE GROUPS

The Choice Groups option allows you to separate your choices into groups, both visually, and also for the purpose of randomization and choice selection.

To add a new Choice Group, click the **purple gear button** to the left of the question, and select **Add Choice Group**.

To add a choice to a Choice Group,
1. Click on the answer choice you would like to assign to a group.
2. Click on the **blue arrow** to the right.
3. Select **Assign to Group**.
4. Type a new group name, or select an existing group.

To set choice group options, click on any Choice Group title, and click the **blue arrow** to the right. The following options are available -
- **HIDE GROUP TITLE:** Remove the title so the participant sees the choices without the group name.
- **MOVE UP AND MOVE DOWN:** Move the entire Choice Group up or down in the choice order.
- **SELECTION:** Select whether to accept a single answer for the entire question, multiple answers for the entire question, a single answer within the choice group (regardless of what is selected outside of the group), or multiple answers within the choice group (regardless of what is selected outside of the group).
- **RANDOMIZATION:** Select whether to use the question's overall randomization settings, to do no randomization within the group (regardless of how the question randomization is set), or to randomize the order of all choices within the group (regardless of how the question randomization is set).

Additional Question Options

Renumber your questions after you finish building your questionnaire. Useful because in Survey Options, you can choose to display this number to the respondents.

These options don't fall under the Advanced Question Options menu, but they are important options to be aware of. These are found in Advanced Options drop-down in the upper right corner of the *Edit Survey* tab.

SURVEY PREVIEW MODE

Survey Preview Mode is selected by default. Unchecking this option changes the editing view. You shouldn't ever need to uncheck this option. It is, however, nice to be aware of its availability if you have difficulty loading the page for any reason.

STRIP FORMATTING

Selecting this option removes any extra formatting from question and answer choice text on selected questions. This is the equivalent of clicking **Remove Formatting** while editing question text or **Remove Format** (eraser icon) in the Rich Content Editor, but on a much larger scale.

You must have questions selected in order to use this option. You can select as few or as many questions as you want.

AUTO-NUMBER QUESTIONS

Every question has a number, or export tag, that appears to its left. As you move questions around and insert questions in between existing questions, the numbers get out of order. Rather than edit the export tags manually (unless you have a very specific type of numbering you would like to use), click the **Auto-Number Questions** option and the system will re-number the questions automatically (Figure 4-11).

This feature renumbers the current questions, but if questions are moved or if more are added, the numbers will get out of order again. You may want to renumber your questions when you get done with all your editing in the survey.

Figure 4-11 Auto-Number Questions dialog

AUTO-NUMBER OPTIONS

- **SEQUENTIAL NUMBERING:** Renumbers questions one-by-one, starting from one until the very last question.
- **BLOCK NUMBERING:** Assigns a number to each block, then assigns a secondary number to each question within that block. Question numbering in each block restarts at one.
  Example: [Block #].[Question #].
- **INTERNAL ID NUMBERING:** Uses the question ID in Qualtrics to keep track of the questions in your survey. Odds are that if you've been editing your survey, your Internal ID Numbering will not end up in alpha-numeric order.
- **PREFIX:** The default is "Q" for "Question", but you can change your prefix and use any number or letter there (no punctuation allowed). You may enter up to four characters, or even remove the prefix and just display numbers without a prefix.

CHECK SURVEY ACCESSIBILITY

Known by many as 508 Compliance, survey accessibility refers to how usable your survey is for someone using a screen reader application. This feature's sole purpose is to help you make your survey friendlier to screen reader applications, and subsequently, to those using the applications.

Help optimize your survey according to 508 Compliance for anyone using a screen reader application.

Check Survey Accessibility is similar to using Spell Check. Clicking this option scans through your survey and makes suggestions about areas where accessibility improvements can be made, as shown in Figure 4-12. It makes recommendations for question types and options to improve access for those individuals using a screen reader program.

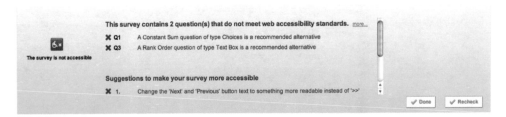

Figure 4-12 Check Survey Accessibility in action.

Most organizations allow survey builders to create non-accessible surveys. There is an **Allow Non-Accessible Surveys** permission enabled by default, which can be disabled at the organization, user type, or user level. If permission changes are needed for your account, please contact the Qualtrics brand administrator at your organization to enable/disable that permission for you.

While Qualtrics does strive for accessibility, certain question types and formats are better suited for accessibility than others. Below is a list showing the different question types and whether they are judged to be accessible.

ACCESSIBLE

- Multiple Choice, all 21 types
- Matrix, except Bipolar
- Text Entry, all
- Side-by-Side
- Rank Order, except Drag and Drop
- Constant Sum, except Slider
- Timing
- Meta
- Descriptive Block
- Drill Down

NOT ACCESSIBLE

- Slider
- Constant Sum Slider
- Matrix Bipolar
- Rank Order Drag and Drop
- Pick, Group, and Rank
- Heat Map
- Hot Spot
- Sliding Scale
- GAP Analysis

Summary

In this chapter we covered some of the more advanced survey building options, including the options you have for adding logic to your survey. Display Logic and Skip Logic are super handy tools that allow you to dictate which respondents see which questions and when. We also went into detail about the Carry Forward and Default Answer Choices options and their use when customizing how respondents interact with your survey.

Additionally, we introduced the option to randomize answer choices. In the tool, the system can randomize the answer choices to prevent display order bias. Later in this book we will go over how you can randomize questions within a block and/or blocks within a survey.

Finally, we covered some of the advanced functions found in the Advanced Options drop-down. It is important to check your survey accessibility if you know you will have respondents that require screen readers or other accessibility tools. The rest of the options in the Advanced Options drop-down menu are more specialized and are covered in Chapter 5, Special Features.

You should now have the knowledge you need to add questions and sophisticated logic to your survey. If you master the ideas in this chapter, you will find that you will be able to collect useful data with greater efficiency.

Chapter 5

Block Options and Survey Flow

The Survey Flow is among the most powerful features in the entire Research Suite. Everything you want to know about it is explained here.

AFTER READING THIS CHAPTER, YOU WILL KNOW HOW TO:

In this chapter you will learn how to:

- Use blocks to organize your survey.
- Use the Survey Flow for advanced logic.
- Randomize Questions within a block and blocks within a survey.
- Use all the Survey Flow elements.

When building your Qualtrics survey, there are many advanced options available that give additional control over your survey questions, your survey logic, and the flow of the questions presented to the respondent. These options won't be needed by everyone all of the time, but the blocks and flow are very useful and powerful tools.

This chapter first provides a discussion on the use of blocks and the available options. Following the introduction to blocks, we then focus on Survey Flow and the tool to make optimal use of the blocks

Blocks and Block Options

When you first create a survey, there is a single default question block inserted for you. This is where you can start inserting your questions. As your survey gets larger and more complicated, you will want to add more blocks to your survey to organize your questions and make it easy to set up which respondents see which questions in your survey. This section will go over all you want to know about blocks and probably more.

QUESTION BLOCKS

Question blocks are used to organize questions by topic, for advanced logic and flow of the survey, and for randomization in the Survey Flow. It's also great for helping to organize your survey when building it.

Question blocks (called Blocks for short), are containers for a group of questions that you create in the Edit Survey tab. For simple surveys, you will probably need only the Default Question Block. If you look just above the first question of your survey, you will see the label Default Question Block.
You can collapse a block by clicking on the down arrow to the left of the Default Question Block label. The view will collapse, showing only the block name and number of questions in the block. Click the block heading bar. The block view will expand to show all questions. This contract-expand feature is useful when managing large surveys. You can open any block you are working on and close all others. You can also rename the block by clicking on the block name and typing in a new name.

More advanced surveys are better served with several blocks of questions. You can create a block for each different question type or category of questions. It is easier to organize and stay on top of your survey when the questions are broken up into smaller bite-sized chunks. More importantly, blocks allow you the flexibility to apply logic options and control each block separately when using Survey Flow and Block Options.

To help understand the power of using blocks, imagine that you create a new product concept test survey with 6 blocks:
- **BLOCK 1:** The introduction and screener block that welcomes respondents and identifies those who are qualified to be respondents.
- **BLOCKS 2 – 4:** The three treatment blocks, one for each product version that will be viewed and evaluated.
- **BLOCK 5:** A demographic questions block.
- **BLOCK 6:** A recruiting block for those interested in providing further feedback about your products - it requests the respondent's email address, and then thanks them for their participation.

Given this block layout, you can easily conceive how you would like to reorder your blocks or add logic to them. Set up in this way, you can decide to only show one of the three treatment blocks to the respondent, randomly display all of them, or set up logic so that they are displayed conditionally.

A block can contain a series of questions, or just a single question. The choice is yours. Creating question blocks will add great power to your ability to do experiments, or just organize the questions within your survey.

The Block Options drop-down menu is located at the top-right corner of the block, and the Survey Flow icon appears in the navigation bar at the top of the edit survey tab.

ADD AND DELETE A BLOCK

You can **Add** a block as an option in the Advanced Options menu (right side of the Edit Survey Bar), or just click on the Add Block button located at the bottom right corner of each question block. Clicking on either will add an additional block at the end of the survey. No need to worry about getting a new block into the Survey Flow; new blocks are automatically added.

Try clicking on **Add Block** and then add a question to that block using the green "+" button to create a new question.

When finished, **delete** the block by selecting Delete in the Block Options menu.

BLOCK OPTIONS

The Block Options menu is found as a drop-down menu at the top-right corner of each question block as shown in Figure 5-1.

Figure 5-1 Block Options.

VIEW BLOCK

At some point, you may want to test out a couple of new questions without having to click through the entire survey to get there. Clicking the **View Block** option is like clicking the Preview Survey button at the top of the page, except it only previews the content of that question block.

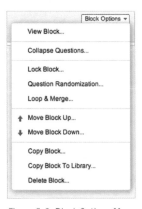

Figure 5-2 Block Options Menu.

COLLAPSE QUESTIONS

The Collapse Questions option minimizes the view of the question to only show the question text in the block and not the answer choices. Like the collapse block option, the collapse question option saves screen real estate when you have a lot of questions in your block and you would like to see a short version of them all. Clicking the option again will expand the questions to full size.

Your question block will automatically collapse when you have a large number of questions in the block (approximately 70+ questions will trigger this). The collapsed questions, or **Large Block** mode helps the page and the questions to load more quickly in large surveys. As noted at the beginning of this chapter, you can expand a block by clicking on the block heading (gray space at top of question block). You can click the **Turn on/off large block mode** to expand the questions view. You also have the option to enter Block Options and unselect the **Collapse Questions** option.

LOCK BLOCK

The Lock Block option (Figure 5-3), as the name implies, locks the question block so it can no longer be edited. You can click **Block Options** and unselect **Lock Block** to edit it again. The idea is to avoid inadvertent editing. Lock Block works like a safety lock you can turn on or off as needed to protect the questions. The Lock Block feature has the option of adding a password (or not) for additional protection.

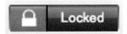

Figure 5-3 Selecting Lock Block places this label on your question block.

QUESTION RANDOMIZATION WITHIN A BLOCK

We've already covered how to randomly present answer choices within a question, but in the Block Options menu you can choose to randomize questions within a block. Question Randomization is one of the more commonly used Block Options. Selecting **Question Randomization** will open a Question Randomization window (Figure 5-4).

Figure 5-4 Question Randomization dialog window.

Blocks with randomization applied to them will display the Randomized Questions icon (Figure 5-5) at the top left, which can be clicked to reopen the Question Randomization dialog.

Figure 5-5 Randomized Questions label.

There are four options in the Question Randomization window:
- **NO RANDOMIZATION:** When selected, nothing is randomized.
- **RANDOMIZE THE ORDER OF ALL QUESTIONS:** Automatically takes all questions and randomizes their order when displayed.

- **PRESENT ONLY __ OF TOTAL QUESTIONS:** Allows you to specify a number of questions to be randomly selected and displayed (4 of 7, 2 of 3, etc.).
- **ADVANCED RANDOMIZATION:** Allows for more control over the randomization options, and you can even combine randomization options (Figure 5-6).
  - *Fixed Display Order:* A subset (or all) questions are selected and the order of presentation is fixed.
  - *Randomize Choices:* Randomizes order of all questions moved into this area.
  - *Randomize Subset:* Specify a number of questions to randomly choose and display (2 of 4, 3 of 7, etc.)
  - *Undisplayed Items:* Specify certain questions you don't want displayed at all.

Figure 5-6 Advanced Randomization dialog.

The up/down arrows for the Fixed Display Order box (Figure 5-6) will change the order of questions. Randomized questions can also be moved using the up/down arrows, and are marked to designate their randomization ({Randomized} and {Random Subset}).

Fixed Display Order is used to predetermine the order of some of the questions. For example, if a question should always appear last, even when you are randomizing other choices, then you can move that question to the bottom of the list in the Fixed Display Order. You can move questions up or down the list by using the up/down arrows.

Use **Questions per Page** to specify how many questions to display at a time. Not specifying a number will randomly display all questions on the same page.

ALERT:
- Using Randomization overrides existing page breaks.
- Randomization also overrides Skip Logic because the question order on the Edit Survey page no longer applies.

LOOP & MERGE

Suppose you have just built a multiple response (check box type) question that states, "Please check up to three car brands you or your family have most recently owned or leased." You have also created a block of questions containing questions about the quality of the automobile that the family owned or leased. Loop and Merge saves you time with this kind of survey.

In this example, Loop and Merge can be used to loop the respondent through the block of evaluation questions for each automobile that they choose. Piped text is used to display the name of the automobile that they are evaluating for each loop. The block will be presented up to three times, once for each car brand selected. The question blocks might read as follows:

"Please reflect on your family's experience with your Ford (and then repeated for Chevrolet and Toyota) and complete the following evaluation:"

This takes the place of creating a separate block for each potential scenario.

Figure 5-7 Loop and Merge label.

There are two Loop & Merge methods:
1. **LOOP AND MERGE OVER QUESTION RESPONSE:** Repeats a block of questions according to each item the participant indicates in a previous question in the survey.
2. **STATIC LOOP AND MERGE:** This is not based off of the participant's selection on a previous question, but on a list of predefined options you provide.

Loop & Merge is logic on steroids. Equivalent to merging a name-address list with the body of a letter. Looping through each and every answer choice selected in a check-box question, you branch to a question block. It can be used with Piped Text and has seriously advanced conditional logic options to control item selection, looping and randomization.

LOOP AND MERGE OVER QUESTION RESPONSE

This option is used to ask the same group of questions about a particular set of selected answers from a previous question. It works by looping through one block of questions multiple times, once for each answer choice selected. This option can greatly reduce survey creation time because the survey creator can ask about each targeted answer choice (brand, occasion, etc.) without having to add the same set of questions to the survey over and over.

Loop and Merge is actually the equivalent of setting up a branch for each choice. The branch then determines if they should enter and see the block of questions or not.

To use the Loop and Merge feature in Qualtrics, you will need two question blocks.

1. Create the first question block and enter the question upon which you want to base your looping. *For example: Which of the following browsers have you used within the last two months? (Select all that apply) Choices: Internet Explorer, Firefox, Safari, Opera, Chrome.*

2. Create the second question block and enter the questions you would like to loop through. *For example: What do you like about this browser?* Since this block will be looped, these questions appear each time the survey loops. In this example, each loop asks about a different browser the respondent has used.

3. In the **Block Options** drop down select **Loop and Merge**, then click **Turn on Loop & Merge**.

4. Select **Automatically bring in Field 1 from a question** (Figure 5-8). If you want to pipe in different text than what is in the answer choice text, then enter text into Field 2 or another column.

5. Select the question serving as the basis for the loop from the first available drop-down menu.

6. In the second drop-down menu, select the condition.
    - **ALL CHOICES:** The looping block will loop for all choices from the target question, selected and not selected.
    - **DISPLAYED CHOICES:** Only loops through the choices that were displayed in the target question. This would only be relevant if you used Display Logic on answer choices in the target question.
    - **UNDISPLAYED CHOICES:** If logic is used to display choices that meet a specific condition, show undisplayed choices.
    - **ALL CHOICES AND ENTERED TEXT:** Will loop through displayed choices plus Other (please specify) text-entry type questions.
    - **SELECTED CHOICES:** The block loops only for responses selected in the target question. Most people choose Selected Choices.
    - **SELECTED CHOICES AND ENTERED TEXT:** Displayed choices plus Other (please specify) type questions.
    - **UNSELECTED CHOICES:** The block loops only for responses **not** selected in the target question.

7. If needed, check one of the advanced options at the bottom.
    a) **RANDOMIZE LOOP ORDER:** The default is to loop the block in the order of the choices selected in the target question. Select this option to randomize that looping order.
    b) **PRESENT ONLY _#_ OF TOTAL LOOPS:** Loop the block only for a specified number of the choices (according to the All Choices, Selected Choices, and Unselected Choices options). This option is only available when Randomize Loop Order is selected.

c) Click the **Save** button.

Figure 5-8 Loop and Merge dialog window.

8. Finally, if you want the respondent to see the item they are currently looping through, you will want to insert piped text code into your questions. To pipe in the answer choice into the looping block:
   a) Click on the **Piped Text Tab**, available when you click on the text of any one of your questions.
   b) Navigate to pipe text from the **Loop and Merge Field**.
   c) Click **Field 1**, or select Field 2 or another field if you've entered text there.
   d) The piped text code will appear and you will want to take the code and put it wherever you would like the item name to appear when the respondent loops.
   e) Repeat steps 1-4 if you have other Field columns to pipe in.

STATIC LOOP AND MERGE

Suppose instead of having the respondent tell you about browsers used, you want to use the same block of questions to ask about the three leading presidential candidates. Since you know you want the questions asked about all of the presidential candidates, you do not need to give the respondent the opportunity to select the candidates in a multiple answer question.

Static Loop and Merge allows you to create a list of items (candidates) or topics to ask about and then loop through them. The system loops as many times as there are items in the list. The item text is piped into the questions for the survey taker. Unlike the other loop and merge, it is static because it is not based off selected choices in a previous question.

To set up a static loop and merge:

1. Click **Block Options** and select **Loop and Merge**.
2. Click Turn On **Loop & Merge**.
3. Do not select **Automatically bring in Field 1 from a question**. In the Field columns, enter fields and values to pipe into your questions (Note: Four fields are referenced here, Field 1, Field 2, Field 3, Field 4, but all four are not required). Example values: Candy Bar, Mars, Snickers, Rolos.
4. Determine if you want to use randomization options.
   - **RANDOMIZE LOOP ORDER:** Displays loop elements in a random order.
   - **PRESENT ONLY _#_ OF TOTAL LOOPS:** Choose a random subset of the possible fields. This is only available when Randomize loop order is selected.
5. Click the **Save** button.
6. Carry out step 8 from the Loop and Merge Over Question Responses instructions to pipe in the field.

Q - T I P

Data is exported as if a separate block of questions were created for each of the possible options. That is because using this option is the equivalent of setting up a specific question block for each possible response on the previous question.

For this reason, using loop and merge can increase the size of your data export greatly. Typically this is only an issue when downloading raw data exports into Excel or SPSS, where there is a column limit (Excel 2003: 256 columns; Excel 2007+: 16,000 columns). If you exceed the limit of Excel, the best option is to download groups of questions at a time rather than the entire survey all at once.

MOVE BLOCK UP

Just as it sounds, selecting this option will move the block up one spot. It actually will switch positions with the block above it.

Performing this action is the equivalent of going into the Survey Flow and moving the block element up one spot (either by clicking and dragging **Move**, or by using the up/down keys on the keyboard).

MOVE BLOCK DOWN

Now on the reverse, selecting this option will move the block down one spot. It actually will switch positions with the block below it.

Performing this action is the equivalent of going into the Survey Flow and moving the block element down one spot (either by clicking and dragging **Move**, or by using the up/down keys on the keyboard).

COPY BLOCK

Copy Block creates an exact replica of the original block. A new question block is created with all of the questions copied and placed within it. The new block is placed at the end of the Edit Survey page, below the existing blocks.

COPY BLOCK TO LIBRARY

The **Copy Block to Library** option allows you to copy an entire block full of questions to your Question Library. You can choose which library to copy the questions to, which category to put them in (optional), and then specify a description for each question. Once you click **Copy**, a copy of each question appears in the selected Question Library.

Figure 5-9 Copy Block to Library dialog window.

DELETE BLOCK

Clicking **Delete Block** in the Block Options drop-down menu will bring up a confirmation dialog window (Figure 5-10). Click **Delete** to confirm and all questions within the block are moved to the Trash/Unused Questions block and the block is removed from the Survey Flow.

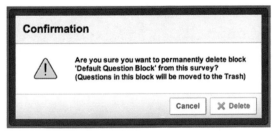

Figure 5-10 Confirmation dialog window.

⇜ Survey Flow

Advanced surveys and experiments require control of the survey flow and better manipulation of the question blocks. Use logic and randomization, or even custom termination points for respondents who don't qualify to continue.

When you're serious about creating advanced surveys, you will be using the Survey Flow, found in the *Edit Survey* Navigation bar (Figure 5-11). Have you ever wanted multiple paths in your survey? Or to display different messages to your qualifying respondents and your non-qualifying respondents? Survey Flow allows you to insert elements into the flow that perform advanced logic, randomization, survey termination messages, and much more to direct the path of the respondent through the survey.

Figure 5-11 *The Survey Flow button.*

The elements that can be inserted into the Survey Flow include (Figure 5-12):

- **BLOCK:** Referring to the question blocks on the main Edit Survey tab, when you select to insert a block element, a block is automatically added to the Survey Flow. Blocks can be added to repeat showing the block in the survey (or show them to different respondents who are guided to different parts of the Survey Flow). You can also reinsert them after a temporary removal.

- **BRANCH:** Similar to Display Logic, but Branch encompasses much more than just one individual question. Using Branch, you can conditionally display blocks or any other Survey Flow element.

- **EMBEDDED DATA:** Using this element you can specify which of your existing embedded data fields you want displayed in your data set. You can even assign embedded fields to individuals.

- **RANDOMIZER:** When elements are placed under the randomizer, the elements are randomly displayed. "Evenly Present Elements" turns this randomizer into a sequencer (sequentially present items). This is useful when displaying a subset of elements in the Randomizer.

- **WEB SERVICE:** Probably the most advanced tool in the Survey Flow. Using the web service, you can send information needing evaluation to an external server. The external server responds with information you can then display or base logic off later in the survey.

- **AUTHENTICATOR:** Requires users to log into your survey, essentially telling the tool who they are. It's great for direct-mail campaigns or scenarios where you might not have an email address. This then links to their panel information for logic, data analysis and piped text.

- **END OF SURVEY:** Typically used in conjunction with a branch, this is useful for early termination of certain non-qualifying respondents. It can be customized to display a certain message, redirect to a URL, and much more. Whenever someone reaches an end of survey element in the survey flow, they are taken to the end of the survey.

- **TABLE OF CONTENTS:** With a Table of Contents, participants are able to switch between Blocks and answer questions in any order they please, instead of needing to go in the order you set. Note that this feature is not available for all Qualtrics accounts. Contact your Account Representative for more information.

- **CONJOINT:** The Research Suite contains a conjoint module (self-explicated method). When you set up a conjoint, the conjoint module is automatically added at the end of the Survey Flow and you must use the Survey Flow to specify where and when it is displayed.

HANDLING THE SURVEY ELEMENTS

Now that you understand the elements that can be added to the Survey Flow, we will briefly identify how to use these
elements.

INSERT ELEMENT

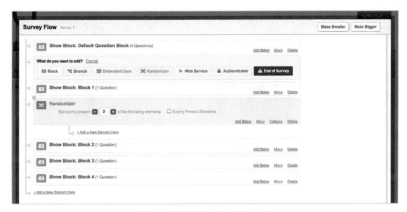

Figure 5-12 Add a New Element.

To **Insert** elements into the Survey Flow:
1. Click **Add a New Element Here** or **Add Below (green text)**.
    - **Add a New Element Here** is a link displayed at the end of the Survey Flow and underneath each Branch, Randomizer, and Authenticator.
    - **Add Below** appears on each element, allowing you to insert an element directly between that element and the one below it.
2. Choices appear in the yellow box. Select the element you would like to insert (Figure 5-12).

Remember that blocks are automatically inserted into the Survey Flow when created in the Edit Survey view.

- Deleting a question block will remove it so respondents won't see it, but it does not actually delete the block of questions. They still remain available on the Edit Survey page.

MOVE ELEMENT

There are two methods you can use to Move elements to the desired position in the Survey Flow:
1. **Move** button (typically used when moving larger distances)
   a. Click and hold the **Move** button on the element. The selected element turns green.
   b. Drag and drop the element at desired location (between or within certain elements).
2. **Up/Down** keys on keyboard (typically used when moving shorter distances)
   a. Click on the element's box to select it (outlines in blue when selected).
   b. Press up or down arrow keys on keyboard to change position.

When moving a branch, randomizer or authenticator, all elements that are nested under it will move as well.

DELETE ELEMENT

To **Delete** or remove elements from the Survey Flow:
1. Press the **Delete** button (every element has a red Delete button on it).
2. When confirmation window displays, click **OK** or **Yes**.

When deleting a branch, randomizer, or authenticator, all elements contained underneath it are removed as well.

COLLAPSE / EXPAND VIEW OF NESTED ELEMENTS

The branch, randomizer and authenticator elements can have other elements nested underneath them. For example, if you would like to randomize blocks , you would place them under a randomizer element.

On these elements, you will also find the Collapse view option.
To **Collapse** or **Expand** the view of an element (for elements containing other elements):
1. Select **Collapse** to collapse elements.
2. Select **Expand** to expand and see all contained elements.

Clicking the "-" and "+" button at the top left corner of the element will also collapse/expand these elements.

RE-SIZE THE SURVEY FLOW VIEW

Change the Size of the Survey Flow view by using the **Make Smaller** and **Make Bigger** buttons at the top right of the Survey Flow window to adjust the size. Make Smaller comes in handy when you need to view more of the Survey Flow at once to get a better feel for your Survey Flow. Make Bigger becomes useful when wanting to return the Survey Flow to its original size.

SAVE SURVEY FLOW

When **Finished** working in the Survey Flow, always remember to click the **Save Flow** button (located at the bottom right). Unlike the main *Edit Survey* tab, your changes are *not* automatically saved.

HOW TO USE THE SURVEY FLOW ELEMENTS...

BLOCK

Click the Block option when inserting an element, then select the block you would like to insert. Repeat this each time you need to insert a block. Each block created on the *Edit Survey* tab is automatically inserted into the Survey Flow.

Figure 5-13 Block Survey Flow element.

Branch is like applying Display Logic to an entire question block or other flow elements. It's useful for experiments and advanced questionnaires.

ALERT: If respondents see the same block multiple times in a survey, they will see each question with their previous responses selected. They are essentially getting the opportunity to answer the questions again, overwriting their previous answers. If you need to have them provide separate responses, then copy the block (*Edit Survey* tab > Block Options) and use the copied block to subsequently "repeat" the block.

BRANCH

Each branch has the Add a New Element Here option beneath it, allowing you to insert elements within the branch. You can also move existing items directly into the branch (see the previous section on moving

Survey Flow elements). These are the items the respondent will see only if they meet the condition specified on the branch.

Figure 5-14 Branch Survey Flow element with condition.

Click **Add a Condition** to specify the criteria that must be met for the items under the branch to be shown. You can base your logic off questions, embedded data, and quotas. Click on the condition to edit the logic statements. When editing, there are +/- buttons to the right of each line of logic to add additional lines of if-then logic and to remove lines of logic, as needed.

Branch conditions are an if-then style of logic; **If** the logic is met, **then** show what is in the branch. This is similar to Display Logic, but different in that you can include any Survey Flow element within the branch, including other branches.

Shift+click the "+" button on your logic to get "And If" logic, which is like having additional parentheses in place within your condition.

EMBEDDED DATA

Add CRM data to your survey. Useful for referencing additional information uploaded with a panel, or for assigning an embedded data field to someone while they take the survey.

Embedded Data (Figure 5-15) is extra information, usually about the respondent, that can be included in the panel and attached to the respondent's data. You can also assign embedded data to respondents through the Survey Flow. If you put in an embedded data field into the Survey Flow and assign a value to it, and the respondent takes a path in the flow through that embedded data, they will be assigned that embedded data value.

Figure 5-15 Embedded Data Survey Flow Element.

Embedded data can be used for in-survey logic (Display and Branch Logic), as well as to filter data and reports. Embedded Data can include extra information like state, city, address, etc., or an identification code. This information is stored with the survey response.

EMBEDDED DATA IN THE SURVEY FLOW

The Embedded Data element is obtained in two ways in the Survey Flow:

1. Obtained from a panel or a survey URL. Specifying which embedded data fields to display in the results (passed from panel or URL).
2. Assigning embedded data variables to the respondent as they are taking the survey based on logic (how someone responds to questions, etc.).

For the embedded data from your panel to be seen in your survey results, you need to put an embedded data element into your Survey Flow and enter each embedded data field name you want to see.

When pulling embedded data from a panel or survey link, it doesn't matter where the element is placed in the Survey Flow. It only matters where you put the embedded data element if you are assigning the field AND value of the embedded data in the Survey Flow. When pulling from a panel, you just need to make sure there is an embedded data element somewhere in the flow.

To Add Embedded Data From a Panel
1. Insert an **Embedded Data Element** into the Survey Flow
2. Define the panel by clicking **Add From Panel** and select the panel. Data fields will appear, click **OK**.
3. **Value will be set from Panel or URL** to the right of embedded data field means the value of the field will be pulled from the embedded data fields in the panel you uploaded, or from the URL (if appending information onto the end of the survey link).
4. **Set a Value Now** does not apply here. It applies to the scenario (below) where you assign a value on the fly.

To enter additional fields, click **Add a New Field**. Any fields you add will be assigned to the respondent at the same time. So if you have different locations for assigning different fields, then insert another Embedded Data element for that particular field and place the element where it's needed within the flow. With panels, there is no need to specify the value. This is automatically taken care of when the field name is entered.

To assign Embedded Data Fields on the Fly:
1. Insert an Embedded Data element.
2. Type the name of the embedded data field where it shows **Enter Embedded Data Field Name Here**.
3. Click **Set a Value Now** to enter in a value that the embedded data will equal.

After setting up the embedded data with the value assigned in the Survey Flow, anyone who passes through the embedded data field will be assigned that value.

ALERT: Location of the Embedded Data element in the Survey Flow is *very important* when you are using it for display or branch logic. Make sure you place this embedded data element where it will assign at the correct time and place. If you are branching and want to assign an embedded data with value to the person who goes through that branch, then add the embedded data element under the branch. The respondent won't see it, but they will be assigned the value.

RANDOMIZER

Just like randomizing questions or answer choices, you can control error by randomizing the presentation order of question blocks and other Survey Flow elements.

The Randomizer is a very useful tool in experimental design. Randomize the display of any element you put under the Randomizer. By default, it will randomize the display order of all elements within the randomizer.

Figure 5-16 Randomizer Survey Flow Element.

To randomly display elements using the Randomizer element:

1. Choose the **Randomizer** element.
2. Move elements underneath the Randomizer, dropping them where it says **Add a New Element Here**.
   - If you would like to randomly display only a subset of the elements under the randomizer, then click the +/- buttons where it says, Randomly present __ of the following elements. If you have 5 elements and choose to randomly present 2, then each time a respondent takes the survey the tool will choose 2 elements out of the 5 to randomly present to the respondent.
   - In this situation, you might consider selecting the **Evenly Present Elements** option to make sure each element gets seen an even amount of times.

EVENLY PRESENT ELEMENTS

Balanced experimental designs require equal numbers of respondents when randomly presenting some of the total number of elements in the Randomizer.

This simple tool on the Randomizer keeps track of how frequently each item has been displayed. If one item has been displayed more than another item, the system will try to even it out by showing the lesser shown items more often to respondents. This turns the Randomizer into somewhat of a sequencer.

Figure 5-17 Evenly Present Elements options.

To enable Evenly Present Elements, select **Evenly Present Elements** on the Randomizer. Once enabled, a **Reset** button appears. When clicked, it displays the options shown in the following screenshot (Figure 5-16).

You can reset all the counts, returning the counts to "0" or you can manually click on the count numbers to change them.

Evenly Present Elements does not need to be used when displaying all elements, as opposed to just a subset, for which it is designed.

WEB SERVICE

The Web Service is an advanced Survey Flow element for advanced logic and data processing. You can send a request to an external server, which houses a script that evaluates data you send over. Once evaluated, the server's script responds with information that is seen by the Qualtrics system as embedded data. You can reference the processed information as embedded data in logic, display it to the respondent, or access it in your post-data-collection analysis.

You can use the Web Service to set up a random number generator, set up a time series, pull in headlines from a website and much more.

To use the Web Service element:
1. Paste the link to the external script into the **URL** field.
2. Click **Add a parameter to send to web service...** to specify parameters to pass to the script.
3. Enter the parameters to pass to the script (For example, max and min values for a random number generator script). Click the "+" to add additional parameters. Click the "-" to remove parameters.
4. Click **Add Embedded Data** to specify how the returned values will be stored as embedded data. *Example:* [embedded data field name] = [return value from script]

Truly dynamic surveys needing advanced computational capabilities can access a Web Service to send data from your survey to a script running on another server. That script can then return a result you can display in the survey or use in logic.

Go to Qualtrics.com/University in your web browser and enter "Random Number Generator" in the search field. You will be able to view an example of a random number generator delivered from a Web Service element.

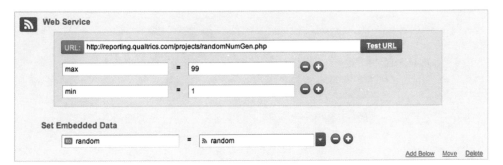

Figure 5-18 Web Service Survey Flow element set up as a Random Number Generator.

AUTHENTICATOR

Proprietary surveys require the ability to check potential respondents against a panel to see if they should be allowed to enter and take the survey. Really useful for highly controlled surveys. It's also useful when doing a direct mail campaign or panel study where you can reference embedded data.

The Authenticator is an interesting tool. Panel members can authenticate against information you already have, essentially telling the Qualtrics Survey Research Suite who they are. It requires the respondent to sign into the survey and once they are signed in, the system will know who they are and be able to assign panel information to their response. This is useful when you have information about the respondent but are not in a situation to send out a unique link through our mailer.

You can choose to have the respondent sign in with their name, email address or any other information you may have on file for them. The respondent tells the tool who they are and they enter the Authenticator (like a branch) and see the elements of the survey.

To set up an Authenticator element, do the following:

1. Import a panel into the Panels tab. An email address is not required. See Chapter 8: Panels for more information on how to do this.
2. Go to the Survey Flow (Edit Survey tab) and insert an **Authenticator**.
3. Select a **Panel**. Start with the **Select Library** drop-down, then select panel name.
4. Specify the fields to authenticate against. Click "+" to add additional fields and "-" to remove fields.
   - Click the **blue arrow** to select the field, or start typing the field name (it will recognize what you type).
   - Select unique fields or a unique combination, like first and/or last name, username, password, phone number, or email address.

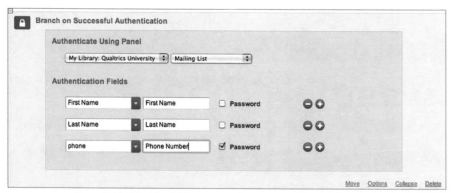

Figure 5-19 Select the fields you would like to authenticate with.

5. If needed, type the **Optional Label** for each field. Use this to make sure fields display how you want them to display to the respondent. For example "First Name" defaults to "RecipientFirst-Name."
6. Select the **Password** checkbox if you want text entered into that field to appear as dots/asterisks, as is custom when entering your password when logging into email or banking sites.
7. Click Options to further customize the Authenticator. Here are the options provided:
   - **MAXIMUM AUTHENTICATION ATTEMPTS:** The number of times potential respondents can fail authentication before they are shown the "Too Many Failures Error" text. The default setting is 3, but you can increase or decrease it as needed.

- **AUTHENTICATION PROMPT TEXT:** The first text you display to the potential respondent when they are asked to authenticate. The default text is, "Please log in." Click the button to select other text or provide your own text to display.
- **AUTHENTICATION ERROR TEXT:** Shown each time the potential respondent fails to authenticate correctly. The default says, "Unable to log in with the information provided." Click the button to select other text or provide your own text to display.
- **TOO MANY FAILURES ERROR TEXT:** When someone fails authentication the amount of times you specified in Maximum Authentication Attempts, they see this message. The default is "Too many failed log-in attempts. Click next to continue." Click the button to select other text or provide your own text to display.
- **ALLOW AUTHENTICATING RESPONDENTS TO RETAKE AUTHENTICATED SECTION:** Choose this only if you want to allow respondents to be able to take the survey again (the authenticated section). Typically, you don't want this option selected.
- **RELOAD ANY PREVIOUSLY SAVED PROGRESS UPON AUTHENTICATION:** If someone can't complete the survey in one sitting, this allows them to later click the link to authenticate again. The survey returns to where they left off (much like using the individual link from the Email Survey page). Typically, this is an option you do want selected.

8. Click the **OK** button to save specified Options.
9. In the Survey Flow, add or move elements under the Authenticator (typically blocks). Any elements that do not go under the Authenticator element will be able to be accessed without a log-in.

Typically, the Authenticator is placed at the very beginning of the Survey Flow. It's the first thing seen and is used to control whether or not one can enter the survey.

END OF SURVEY

Using this element, you can specify different ways to terminate the survey for your respondents. Typically, this element is placed within a branch (Figure 5-20) in order to only terminate those who do or do not match certain criteria, but you can also place one at the end of the flow to give a custom end of survey message or redirect your respondents.

Customize the message seen at the end of the survey or show the respondent a report of their responses.

Figure 5-20 End of Survey Element within a Branch.

There are a lot of useful ways to customize an End of Survey element. Click Customize to see the following customization options:

- **DEFAULT END OF SURVEY MESSAGE:** When selected, the default selection displays a message that says, "We thank you for your time spent taking this survey. Your response has been recorded."

- **REDIRECT TO SINGLE RESPONSE REPORT:** Select if you want to display to the survey taker a report of their response, allowing them to download it as a PDF. This is the same report you see on the Responses (Recorded Responses) page of the tool when clicking the Response ID.

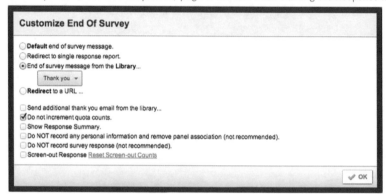

Figure 5-21 Customization options available when Customize button is clicked.

- **END OF SURVEY MESSAGE FROM THE LIBRARY:** Display your own custom message to your survey-takers. Select an existing message from your message library or create a new one.

- **REDIRECT TO A URL:** Redirect participants to another URL when they finish the survey, like your organization's website. Simply copy/paste the URL into the text field.

- **SEND ADDITIONAL THANK YOU EMAIL FROM THE LIBRARY:** Send a Thank You email to your participants who complete your survey, one by one as their responses come in. This only affects those who terminate at this specific End of Survey element. Select an existing Thank You message or create a new one.

- **DO NOT INCREMENT QUOTA COUNTS:** Don't increment quota counts for respondents who terminate at the specific End of Survey element. Quota counts only increment when someone terminates the survey, but typically you don't want to increment the count for someone who doesn't qualify for your survey.

- **SHOW RESPONSE SUMMARY:** Displays a respondent's survey questions with the buttons/checkboxes selected. This allows the respondent to download it as a PDF. It is very similar to Redirect to single response report, but this report has a design template similar to the survey.

- **DO NOT RECORD ANY PERSONAL INFORMATION AND REMOVE PANEL ASSOCIATION (NOT RECOMMENDED):** Check this option to make sure responses are anonymous. If coming from a panel, respondents who reach this element will not have their response associated with their name, email address, or embedded data from the panel. They will appear as an anonymous response, as if they had clicked the Anonymous Survey Link. This is not recommended because once the association is removed, it cannot be recovered. If you select this, make sure it is a feature you want to use.

- **DO NOT RECORD SURVEY RESPONSE (NOT RECOMMENDED):** Will not count certain responses that pass over this element. This is especially useful if your license has a restriction on how many responses it can have. Using this option you can count just those who qualify for your survey. This is not recommended because you're telling the tool to not store certain responses. These cannot be recovered if not recorded. Be sure this is a feature you want to use before selecting it.

- **SCREEN-OUT RESPONSE:** Use this option to tally respondents who leave the survey at this point in the Survey Flow without actually saving their responses. A new Screen-Out Report table will be available in Reporting Beta showing how many participants were screened out at your different End of Survey points. Note that this feature is not available for all Qualtrics accounts. Contact your Account Representative for more information.

Most of these options are also available in the Survey Termination area of Survey Options, which lets you specify default end of survey behavior for when no other action is specified in Survey Flow.

TABLE OF CONTENTS

With a Table of Contents, participants are able to switch between Blocks to answer questions in any order they please, instead of needing to go in the order you set. Note that this feature is not available for all Qualtrics accounts. Contact your Account Representative for more information.

To set up a Table of Contents,

1. Add a Table of Contents element anywhere into the Survey Flow (typically the very beginning of the flow is appropriate)
2. Move any needed blocks or branches into the Table of Contents (see the previous section on moving Survey Flow elements).
3. On any question blocks that should be mandatory, check the box for "Table of Contents: Force respondents to finish the block".

Figure 5-22 Table of Contents Options

4. Click **Options** on your Table of Contents element to see the following settings -

- **ADD TABLE OF CONTENTS INTRODUCTION MESSAGE:** This allows you to specify an introduction message to show respondents at the beginning of the survey.
- **ADD TABLE OF CONTENTS CONCLUSION PAGE:** At the end of the survey, the Table of Contents will display again showing which question blocks have and have not been answered, allowing the respondent to jump to the unanswered blocks, as well as back to the answered ones. You have the option to display the default message or select your own message from the library.
- **SHOW SIDEBAR:** Display a Table of Contents sidebar that is persistent throughout the survey, so participants can switch between blocks at any point.
- **SHOW BLOCK PROGRESS:** In the Table of Contents sidebar, a percentage is placed next to each question block so participants can see their progress in each section.
- **SHOW BUTTON:** Allows you to include a Table of Contents button on every page so the respondent return there at any point in the survey.

CONJOINT

Conjoint Analysis is a technique used to assess the relative importance individuals place on different features of a given product. A conjoint study usually involves showing respondents a set of features and asking them to indicate how much they like or prefer the different attributes of that feature.

For example, the acceptability of an assortment of yet undeveloped new product configurations could be evaluated using the attribute configurations that define the products. To read more about conjoint analysis go to Qualtrics.com/University.

The conjoint option only displays if a conjoint question is built. Discussion of building the conjoint question type is contained in Chapter 6: Special Features. Once inserted, just place the conjoint in the Survey Flow where you need it to appear to the respondent. The Qualtrics conjoint analysis element uses the self-explicated model approach (Srinivasan and Park, Journal of Marketing Research, May 1997). Other approaches to conjoint analysis, like choice based and max-diff, will need to be built separately within the survey.

Figure 5-22 Conjoint Survey Flow Element.

See the Conjoint area under Chapter 6: Special Features for more information on setting up a conjoint.

Summary

Phew! You made it to the end of Chapter 5. You now know almost everything there is to know about building a survey in the Research Suite. In this chapter we went over the importance of blocks in organizing your survey and preparing for the use of advanced logic in the Survey Flow. We also covered how to use branches in the Survey Flow to guide respondents through different paths in the survey depending on their responses to previous questions.

After reading this chapter you should have a good idea of what all of the elements are in the Survey Flow and what they do. The Branch, Randomizer, Embedded Data and End of Survey elements are the ones you will use the most, so spend some time getting to know them. You will be amazed at the research you can pull off when you combine blocks and Survey Flow elements to create a complex survey.

Chapter 6

Special Features

If you're doing a unique study, this is the chapter for you. We've built many special features for the world's leading researchers. This chapter explains how to use them all.

IN THIS CHAPTER YOU WILL LEARN ABOUT:

- Triggers
- SalesForce Integration
- Quotas
- Translate Survey
- Scoring
- Test Survey
- Import/Export Survey

This chapter presents seven special features that are useful in certain circumstances. These options are all available in the *Edit Survey* tab under the **Advanced Options** drop-down menu. If you don't know what triggers are, or whether scoring could be useful to you, read over this chapter and you may find that these special features are exactly what you need to make your survey and reporting great.

✿ Triggers

Receive sales leads, customer complaints, Sarbanes Oxley notifications. Trigger an email when someone responds a certain way. You can even email respondents with their responses as a survey completion confirmation.

Two types of triggers are available in Qualtrics. Type one, email triggers, allows you to send an email notification when a certain event occurs. Type two, panel triggers, allows you to add a respondent's name to a panel you are building. Triggers are often used in conjunction with customer and website feedback surveys that report highly dissatisfied customers. If the company wants to engage in customer retention efforts, they can immediately know the results of their surveys and make the needed changes.

Similarly, triggers are useful when distributing feedback from whistleblower surveys, as prescribed under Sarbanes-Oxley legislation. Finally, if you are collecting sales leads through product interest surveys, you can easily have triggers sent to the appropriate sales team. In each of these cases, a key person receives an email and has the information to immediately take action to recover the customer, minimize damage, or make a sale.

EMAIL TRIGGERS

The **Email Triggers** option sends an email message when a specified condition or event occurs (Figure 6-1). This means that the Qualtrics system can alert you or someone else when someone answers a survey in a particular way. For example, if you're running a customer satisfaction survey, you may want to know if someone mentions they were dissatisfied with their experience. You can get this alert straight to your inbox or smartphone as soon as a response is completed with a dissatisfied answer. Likewise, a new sales lead can be instantly delivered to your inbox, allowing you to make a faster response, just when the prospective customer is at the peak of their interest in your product or company.

Figure 6-1 Email trigger window.

TO CREATE AN EMAIL TRIGGER:

1. Under the Advanced Options drop-down, hover over Triggers and select **Email Triggers**.
2. By default, the Trigger will send an email when a survey is completed. However, if you want to receive only a specific category of email, click the **Add a Condition** link located above the Email address box.
    - Set up the condition.
        - Logic can be based off of Question selections, Embedded Data, and/or Quotas.
        - The "+" can be used to create additional lines of logic conditions with the AND and OR operators.
        - Shift+clicking the "+" will create an "AND IF" statement, equal to parentheses for more advanced logic. Change this to "OR IF" by clicking on the "AND IF" text.
3. Now fill in the fields with the necessary information for your trigger: "To" email address; "From" email address; Subject line; Message.
4. Choose when you want the email to be sent. Most often you will want to send immediately, but you have the option to delay the mailing from **1 hour** to **28 days**.
5. **Include Response Report** means that a simple report summarizing the triggering participant's response will be sent as part of the email body. Enabled by default, uncheck this option if you prefer not to include this report.
6. Click **Save Triggers** or **Finish Editing** if you would like to move on to building another Email Trigger.

When a respondent completes a survey, the email trigger is sent if the specified condition is met.

An email address can be piped in from an answer choice. To learn how to do this, see Insert Piped Text in the Advanced Choice Options chapter.

PANEL TRIGGERS

Automatically create a panel from your survey respondents. You can even set a condition so the panel contains people matching a certain criteria.

Panel triggers are a great way to build a customer panel. You can add an individual to a panel or update an existing panel member (Figure 6-2). This is especially useful when you want to create your own panel, and allows you the flexibility of only including those who opt into your panel. You can request contact information in an initial survey and have that information automatically inserted into a panel that you can use to send out a second survey.

Just like the email trigger, the panel trigger performs only when the specific conditions that you specify are met.

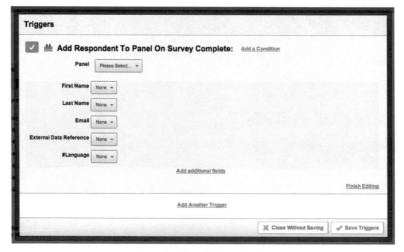

Figure 6-2 Panel trigger window.

TO CREATE A PANEL TRIGGER:
1. Under the Advanced Options drop-down, hover over Triggers and select **Panel Triggers**.
2. By default, the Panel Trigger is set to include the individual in the panel upon survey completion. To create or update panel members based on certain criteria, click **Add a Condition**.
   - Logic can be based upon Question selections, Embedded Data, and Quotas.
   - The "+" can be used to create AND and OR operators.
   - Shift+clicking the "+" will create an "AND IF" statement, equal to parentheses for advanced logic. Change this to "OR IF" by clicking on the "AND IF" text.
3. Select the Library and Panel into which you would like to place your new panel members. If you don't have a panel already created, see Chapter 8 on Panels to learn how to create a new panel in the Panels tab.
4. Specify which question responses go into the main panel fields: First Name, Last Name, Email External Data Reference, and Language (Select "None" if that specific field is not needed).
5. Click **Add Additional Fields** if you would like to include an additional embedded data field in the panel.
6. Specify the embedded data field name (text box on far left).
7. Choose if you would like to pull the information from a question, embedded data field, or recipient information (e.g., fields containing name, email) by clicking on the drop-down menu.

8. Select the question, embedded data field name, or recipient info field using the next drop-down list.
9. Select the answer choice, if based upon a question. This step does not apply if the logic is based upon embedded data or recipient information.
10. Click **Save Triggers**, or **Finish Editing** if you would like to move on to building another Panel Trigger.

When respondents take the survey, the Panel Trigger will place their information into the panel as long as the condition that you have put in place has been met.

❋ Salesforce

Create and edit Salesforce leads and contacts through links to your survey.

Do you use Salesforce.com? If so, we've got you covered. Salesforce is a powerful Customer Relationship Management (CRM) tool that many organizations use to keep track of sales leads and contacts. Now you can integrate your surveys into Salesforce. Please note that Salesforce Integration is an additional service that is not included with the standard Research Suite packages.

Set Up Link to your Salesforce Account

All Salesforce options, except for Web to Lead, need the survey to be linked up using the Security Token. It's best to set up the link ahead of time.

Figure 6-3 Salesforce Account Login dialog.

TO LINK YOUR QUALTRICS SURVEY TO YOUR SALESFORCE ACCOUNT:

1. Under the Advanced Options menu, navigate to **Salesforce**.
2. Select **Setup Link to Salesforce Account**.
3. Type in your Salesforce User Name, Password, and Security Token.
   To get your Security Token:
   a) Log in to Salesforce.com.

b) Within Salesforce, click your name and select **Setup**.

c) Click **My Personal Information**.

d) Select **Reset My Security Token**.

e) Click **Reset Security Token** button and wait for the email.

f) Copy and paste the Security Token into the appropriate field in the Qualtrics Survey Research Suite.

4. Click **Save**.

Q-TIP

If you are new to Salesforce integration, check the box for **Sandbox Environment**. This allows you to create a carbon copy of your organization and data, placing it in a sandbox. Now you can play around without the worry of messing up your original data.

WEB TO LEAD

The Web to Lead option allows you to pull information from your survey and put it into the Lead object of your Salesforce account. Similar to an Email Trigger or Panel Trigger, you can then set the conditions for which respondents get pulled into Salesforce.

Figure 6-4 Salesforce Web to Lead window.

TO USE THE WEB TO LEAD FEATURE:

1. Under the Advanced Options drop-down menu, hover over **Salesforce**.

2. Select **Web to Lead**.

3. Enter your **Organization ID** from Salesforce. This specifies where lead information is stored.

   To get the Organization ID, log in to salesforce.com.

   a. Within Salesforce click your name and select **Setup**.

b. Select **Administrative Setup**.

c. Click **Company Profile**.

d. Click **Company Information**.

e. Under **Organization Detail** you will find a 15-character alphanumeric value for the Salesforce.com Organization ID (second column toward the bottom).

f. Copy and paste value into the **Organization ID** field in the Web to Lead window.

4. At the top of the window, create a condition for when you'd like the lead to be triggered. Don't specify a condition if you'd like a lead created every time the survey is completed. Conditions can be based upon questions, embedded data fields, and quotas.

5. Use the drop-down menus to guide you through the fields in Salesforce you'd like to populate. This also guides you through choosing a location in the survey from where you'll pull the information. This feature limits you to the standard Lead fields identified by Salesforce. For pulling in additional objects and fields, see the Response Mapping information in the next section. The basic format is the following: [Salesforce Lead field] = [Qualtrics logic type (Question, Embedded Data, Specified Value)].

Example setups:

QUESTION: [Salesforce Lead Field] = Question, select Question, select corresponding answer choice (or answer choice value). This pulls in selected or entered information from a question.

EMBEDDED DATA: [Salesforce Lead Field] = Embedded Data, *enter embedded data field name*. This pulls in assigned information from an embedded data field.

SPECIFIED VALUE: [Salesforce Lead Field] = *Enter static value to assign*. This pulls in static information you want to assign to anyone who triggers this Web to Lead trigger.

6. Use the blue plus and minus signs to the right to add or remove additional "and if" and "or if" conditions to your logic.

7. When finished click **Save**, or **Finish Editing** to add another Web to Lead trigger.

Q-TIP

- To create additional Salesforce triggers, click **Add Another Lead Trigger**. You can set up additional triggers to add different information.

- To test your Web to Lead trigger setup, use the Preview Survey button in the Edit Survey tab. When finished with the survey, a message is provided indicating whether or not the lead was successfully saved into your Salesforce account.

- Check your Salesforce account for verification that the lead has been saved as desired. The lead may not appear for a few minutes as it needs to pass through the Salesforce Web to Lead system before it can appear.

RESPONSE MAPPING TO SALESFORCE

Response Mapping takes the Web to Lead feature a step further. It allows you to automatically insert information from your survey into any object or field of your Salesforce account. Additionally, you can update or remove any existing Salesforce object. Conditions can be set using advanced logic to identify specifically which respondents will be saved, updated or removed. These conditions can be based upon question responses, embedded data fields, or survey quotas.

TO USE THE RESPONSE MAPPING OPTION:

1. Under the Advanced Options menu, navigate to **Salesforce**.
2. Select **Response Mapping**.
   - If you haven't already linked to your Salesforce account, you can do that in the Salesforce Account Login window that appears. Please refer to the beginning of this Salesforce tutorial for step 3 in the Set Up Link to Salesforce Account section.
3. The default setting is for all completed surveys to trigger a lead. Click **Add a Condition** to specify criteria for when someone should trigger a lead.
   - Conditions can be based upon questions, embedded data fields, and quotas. Use the blue plus and minus signs to the right to add or remove additional "and if" and "or if" conditions to your logic.
4. Under the **Action** drop-down, specify the action for the Qualtrics tool to take when the condition is met. These include the ability to **Update**, **Insert**, and **Delete** objects in your Salesforce account. See below for further information explaining how to use the Update, Insert, and Delete options.

TO UPDATE OR DELETE AN OBJECT:

1. Select **Update** or **Delete** under the Action drop-down.
2. Identify the **Salesforce Object** in the drop-down menu.
3. Under the **Salesforce Field to Response Mapping** section, use the drop-down menus to identify the fields to populate in Salesforce. You will also identify the location in the survey from where you'll be pulling the information.
   - Add/remove additional fields to map to your Salesforce account by using the blue plus and minus signs to the right.
4. Select a **Key** in the left-hand column.
   - When updating or deleting, a unique field (the **Key**) is needed to make sure the correct object is changed. The field you specify as the Key is used as the unique identifier to locate the object. If the key is not unique, more than one object can be returned. If more than one object is returned, the action to update or delete will fail and no action will occur.
5. Click **Save**, or select **Finish**, and click **Add Another Response Mapping** to set up additional response mappings.

TO INSERT AN OBJECT:
1. Under the Action drop-down, select **Insert**.
2. Identify the **Salesforce Object** in the drop-down.
3. Under the Salesforce Field to Response Mapping section, use the menus to identify the fields in Salesforce to populate, as well as the location in the survey where you'll be pulling the information from.
    - Add/remove additional fields to map to your Salesforce account by using the blue plus and minus signs to the right.
4. Click **Save**, or select Finish and click **Add Another Response Mapping** to set up additional Response Mappings.

Q - T I P

- Setting up your Response Mapping trigger is just like Web to Lead. Use the Preview Survey button on the Edit Survey tab. When finished with the survey, a message is provided indicating whether or not the lead was successfully saved into your Salesforce account.
- Check your Salesforce account for verification that the lead has been saved as desired. The lead may not appear for a few minutes as it needs to pass through the Salesforce Web to Lead system before it can appear.

TRIGGER AND EMAIL SURVEY

The Trigger and Email Survey option allows you to send an automatic email trigger and trigger a survey that will be sent whenever a specified object's Workflow rule has been met in Salesforce.

To use the Trigger and Email option, you first need a Workflow Rule and Outbound Message set up in Salesforce. To create a Workflow Rule and Outbound Message in Salesforce:
1. Login to Salesforce.com.
2. Within Salesforce, click on your name near the top of the page and select Setup.
3. In the left-hand menu, click **Create** and select **Workflow and Approvals**.
4. Click **Workflow Rule**.
5. Click the **New Rule** button.
6. Select the object to use for your rule.
7. Click **Next** button.
8. Give your rule a name and description.
9. Set your condition for the rule.
10. Click the **Save and Next** button.
11. Set an action for your rule by selecting **New Outbound Message**.
12. Edit the name, description, and from name for the outbound message.
13. Copy the end URL found in the Qualtrics Trigger and Email Survey window and paste it into the outbound URL location in Salesforce.

Figure 6-5 Salesforce Trigger and Email Survey window.

TO USE TRIGGER AND EMAIL SURVEY:

1. Under the **Advanced Options** drop-down, navigate to Salesforce.
2. Select **Trigger** and **Email Survey**.
3. In the dialog window, click **Add an Outbound Message**.
4. Once created, you'll see an option to select a **Salesforce Object and Email Field**.
   - The Object's **Rule** is what triggers the outbound message.
   - The **Email Field** is the email address the message will be sent to.
   - The **Store Email in Panel** option allows you to store that person's information into a panel for future use or for use as embedded data. This is optional, but it is required if you want to use embedded data to pass information from Salesforce into your survey or results.
5. Once a panel is selected, click **Show Available Embedded Data**. The listed fields are the fields you can pass into your survey and use as piped text and save into your results.
6. Enter the **From Name**, **Reply-to Email Address**, and **Subject** for the message to be sent.
7. Click the **Load a Saved Message** drop-down menu and either select a message from your library or create a new one by selecting **New Message** under your library.
8. Copy and paste the **Outbound Message URL** into the endpoint URL for your outbound message in Salesforce. This is the message associated with the workflow rule for the object you selected above.

TO PASS EMBEDDED DATA FROM SALESFORCE TO QUALTRICS

At times it's useful to pull additional information from Salesforce into Qualtrics for reporting purposes.

TO PULL FIELDS FROM SALESFORCE INTO QUALTRICS:
1. Click on the **Advanced Options** drop-down and navigate to Salesforce.
2. Select **Trigger and Email Survey**.
3. In the dialog window, click **Show Available Embedded Data**.
4. Copy the necessary embedded data fields.
    * The right column is the Salesforce field.
    * The field in the left column is the Qualtrics field matching the corresponding Salesforce fields.
5. Paste the **Embedded Data** field IDs as embedded data into your Survey Flow:
    1. Under *Edit Survey*, click **Survey Flow**.
    2. Click **Add a New Element Here** (the position at the bottom is fine).
    3. Select the **Embedded Data**.
    4. Paste the **Embedded Data** field IDs from the list in step 4 into the text fields where it says **Enter Embedded Data Field Name Here**.

TO REFERENCE SALESFORCE FIELDS IN QUALTRICS MESSAGES:
1. Follow steps 1-4 above.
2. In the Rich Content Editor when editing the message, click the **Piped Text** icon {a}.
3. Hover over **Embedded Data**.
4. In the text field, paste the **Embedded Data** field name (from the left column referenced in Step 4 of the above steps).

QUALTRICS ON SALESFORCE APP EXCHANGE

The Salesforce App Exchange enables you to access your Qualtrics account and all of its functionalities within the Salesforce dashboard. It's a free app to all Qualtrics users. For more information on Qualtrics for Salesforce App Exchange, visit http://appexchange.salesforce.com/ and search for "Qualtrics".

❉ Quotas

Also found in the Advanced Options drop-down is the **Quotas** option. The Quotas feature allows you to track the number of responses that match certain criteria and then limit how many people can take part or all of the survey. Once the quota is met, you can terminate the survey, skip a question or block, or deactivate the survey based on the number of specified responses in the quota. As discussed in Chapter 4 of this book, Quotas can be used with the Add Skip Logic option found in the advanced question options (purple gear) to the left of each question.

Quotas can be measured by question response, embedded data, or even another quota (Figure 6-6). The quota feature is useful when you wish to have only a certain number of responses, or when you have several groups and you want a specific number of responses from each group (i.e. equal responses from males and females).

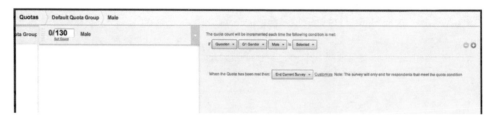

Figure 6-6 Quotas dialog box.

TO CREATE A QUOTA:
1. Click on the Advanced Options drop-down menu and select **Quotas**.
2. In the Quotas box, click **Add a Quota**.
3. Enter a name for the quota.
4. Enter a number for the **Quota Limit**.
   - The Quota Limit is the number of responses required before the specified action (step 6) takes effect.
5. Select the type of quota you want to create, "Simple Logic Quota" or "Cross Logic Quota".
   - Note that Cross Logic is not available for all Qualtrics accounts - if you do not have access, you will be taken directly to the Simple Logic editor. Contact your Account Representative for more information.

FOR SIMPLE LOGIC QUOTAS
6. Set up the quota condition. Every time this condition is met, the quota will be tallied.
   - You can base the condition upon a question response, embedded data, or another quota.
   - This is the same logic box as used in Skip, Display, or Branch Logic and works in the same way.
   - Click the blue + sign to add another condition, or to "Move to a new Logic Set", which allows you to group logic statements together.

FOR CROSS LOGIC QUOTAS

6. Set up the quota condition. Each logic set uses percentages to define how respondents are distributed.
    • For example, if your quota allows for 500 responses, you can set Males to 50% and Females to 50% to get 250 respondents of each.
    • Refer to the Current Respondent Distribution at the bottom to see how your logic sets interact to determine how many respondents with each set of criteria are allowed in the quota.

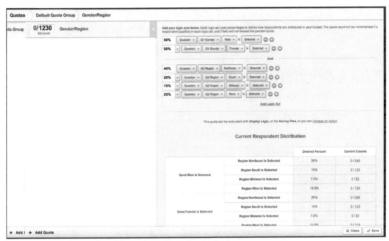

Figure 6-7 Cross Logic Quotas

7. Select an action to take when the quota count is met (quota is full).
    • The default setting is **End Current Survey**, which terminates the individual response for a respondent who comes into the survey and meets the quota condition after the quota count is met. Click **Customize** to the right of the drop-down to edit what the respondent will see if the survey is terminated. These options are the same as those in the End of Survey Element in the Survey Flow. Refer to Chapter 5: Block Options and Survey Flow for a detailed explanation.
    • Qualtrics can deactivate the survey, hide a question or block of questions ("Do Not Display..." options), or leave it to Survey Flow logic. See the additional section below for more information on setting up the quota logic in the Survey Flow. "Do the above action only if the current respondent meets the quota condition" will be available and checked by default if choosing an action other than the default.
8. Click **Save Quotas**, or **Finish Editing** if you would like to create more quotas.

MULTIPLE MATCH HANDLING

If a respondent qualifies to increment more than one quota, you can specify which quota(s) you want to be incremented by their response. Choose to increment all quotas that the respondent qualifies for, just the first or last quota, or the most or least filled quota.

Conjoint Analysis

The conjoint option is a combined data collection and analysis tool. Measuring preferences for products or services, it is actually used to understand how people value the specific features of a product or service.

In the Qualtrics tool, you can add a self-explicated conjoint to your survey (Figure 6-8). The self-explicated model asks respondents direct questions about how much they desire each of a set of attributes or features, and then the model asks respondents to indicate a level of preference for each.

TO SET UP A CONJOINT IN YOUR QUALTRICS SURVEY:

1. Under the Advanced Options drop-down, select **Conjoint**.
2. Click **Add a Conjoint**.
3. The first page shows an explanation of conjoint analysis. When ready, click **Next** to start your conjoint creation.
4. To distinguish this conjoint from others you create, enter a **Name** (top text box) and **Data Export Tag** (bottom text box), then click **Next**.
    - The **Data Export Tag** is used to help identify which fields in the survey results relate to the conjoint.
5. Enter the **Features** for the product or service being tested.

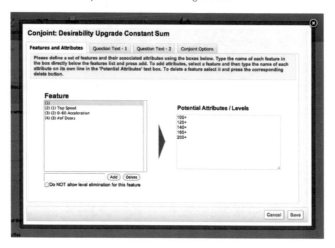

Figure 6-8 Setting up a self-explicated conjoint.

6. Click **Save**.
7. Click **Survey Flow** and place the Conjoint element (light blue) in the correct position in the survey. Remember to click the **Save Flow** button when finished.

TO ADD A FEATURE:

1. Type the name of the feature in the text box below the Feature area.
2. Click **Add**.
3. Choose if you want to allow participants the option to eliminate attributes/levels for the feature. This is done by checking or unchecking the box for **Do NOT allow level elimination for this feature** under the Features list. This is selected by default. If not selected, the **Instructions for elimination of feature** levels question from the Question Text – 1 tab will be asked regarding the attributes/levels of that feature.
4. Enter the Potential Attributes/Levels for the added Features.

Elimination of feature levels implies that you would never buy or use a product with that feature level. In fact, you would rather go without than buy this product configuration. For example, if I were highly allergic to peanuts, I'd rather have no candy bar than one with peanuts.

TO REMOVE A FEATURE:

1. Select a feature in the Feature list.
2. Click **Delete**.

TO ADD ATTRIBUTES/LEVELS FOR A FEATURE:

1. Select the feature in the Features area.
2. Click in the Potential Attributes/Levels box and type in the attributes/levels to include. Insert one per line.

TO REMOVE ATTRIBUTES/LEVELS FOR A FEATURE:

1. Select the feature in the Features area.
2. Click in the Potential Attributes/Levels box and use the backspace or delete key on your keyboard to delete the attribute's text.

TO EDIT THE TEXT OF THE ACTUAL CONJOINT QUESTIONS:

1. Click the **Question Text – 1** tab and review the question text and instructions used. Suggested text is found in each of the question areas. Edit this text to make the questions work better for your study. There are three questions that you will need to write:

   - **INSTRUCTION TEXT FOR ELIMINATION OF FEATURE LEVELS:** These instructions only display if "Do NOT allow level elimination for this feature" is not selected for any features.
   - **INSTRUCTION TEXT FOR SELECTING THE MOST AND LEAST PREFERRED LEVELS:** This is the question text respondents will see when they are asked to select the Least Preferred attribute and Most Preferred attribute from the listed attributes/levels for each feature.
   - **INSTRUCTION TEXT FOR EVALUATING "PREFERENCE" OF LEVELS NOT MOST OR LEAST PREFERRED:** This is always displayed after "Instructions for select most and least preferred

levels." This question asks (using a 0-10 scale) about all remaining attributes that were not the least or most preferred from the previous question.

2. Click **Question Text – 2** tab and review the instruction text used. Edit this text to make the questions work better for your study.

- **INSTRUCTION TEXT FOR MEASURING IMPORTANCE USING CONSTANT SUM QUESTION:** This is the question text for the Constant Sum question. It displays at the end of the conjoint only when Feature Importance Constant Sum is selected on the Conjoint Options tab.
- **INSTRUCTION TEXT FOR MEASURING UPGRADE DESIRABILITY USING CONSTANT SUM QUESTION:** This is the question text for the Constant Sum question displayed at the end of the conjoint. It appears only when Desirability Upgrade Constant Sum is selected on the Conjoint Options tab.

In self-explicated conjoint analysis, the importance scores are used as a multiplier for the preference scores. The **constant sum** method of measuring importance generally gives a broader distribution for the importance scores than does the upgrade desirability method. The **upgrade desirability** method is appropriate when the importance features (a feature is absent or present) are being evaluated.

TO SET CONJOINT OPTIONS:

1. Click the **Conjoint Options** tab to make any changes as needed.

- **NAME FOR CONJOINT ANALYSIS:** You can change the name you provided when first setting up the conjoint.
- **DATA EXPORT TAG:** You can change the Data Export Tag you provided when first setting up the conjoint.
- **CONJOINT DISPLAY OPTIONS:**
  - *Feature Importance Constant Sum:* The Constant Sum question displayed at the end of the conjoint asks for allocation of each feature's most preferred attribute/level based upon percentage.
  - *Desirability Upgrade Constant Sum:* The Constant Sum question displayed at the end of the conjoint asks for 100% allocation for each feature. It is based upon the premise that one is upgrading the product from the respondent's lowest preferred attribute/level (From) to the most preferred attribute/level (To) for the feature.

- Conjoint data does not display in the View Reports area, so data must be downloaded from the **Download Data** page and analyzed in an external application.
- Once your Conjoint is in the correct location, we recommend you click Survey Preview and test your survey with the Conjoint in place.
- This book won't be touching on the analysis side of the conjoint. Go to Qualtrics.com/University to search for conjoint papers, or the Professional Services team at Qualtrics can provide assistance, if needed.

✻ Translate Survey

The Translate Survey tool is a powerful tool that provides a fast start in translating your survey. Within the tool you are given a translator-friendly side-by-side view for entering the translations (Figure 6-9). When the survey is taken by the respondent, the system automatically recognizes the default browser language of the respondent and presents the appropriate survey language. The respondent can also choose the language they would like to take the survey in by selecting it from a drop-down in the upper right hand corner of the survey.

When Translate Survey is used, the survey can be taken in multiple languages and all of the data collected is stored in one place, allowing you to analyze all the data together. If desired, you can view which languages the survey was taken in and take that into consideration when analyzing your data.

Select from more than 40 languages to automatically provide the best-suited translation of your survey to your respondents. All data from the different translations is overlayed into the one survey database.

Figure 6-9 *Translate Survey tool in action.*

TO USE THE TRANSLATE SURVEY TOOL:

1. Select **Translate Survey** under the Advanced Options drop-down.
2. The first time you open the translator, you'll see the first question of your survey on the left-half of the screen, and the right-half of the screen will be blank. Above the right-half of the screen, select **Add a Language**.
3. From the **Survey Languages** list, choose the language translations to add to your survey, and click **Close**.
4. You will now see your default language on the left-half of the editor, and the question text on the right ready to be translated. To begin translating your first question, click on the question text or answer choices and replace the text with the translated text.
5. To switch between questions, click the left and right **Arrows** on the right side of the gray toolbar.
6. To change which translation language you are working on, click on the **Language drop-down** above your translation on the right half of the screen, and choose one of the other languages.

After translating your survey into the desired languages, you can preview your survey and see that in the upper-right hand corner of the survey, there is the option to change between languages. The respondent can click here to change between languages. Also, the system will auto-detect which language their browser is in and display the survey automatically in that language.

Q-TIP

- When putting in the translation, a percentage shows above each question to show you how much of the question has been translated.
- Click the **Toggle Translation Overview** button (icon of two columns) next to the left/right arrows to see a percentage of all translations provided. Click any question's percentage in its language column to jump directly to that question to edit that particular translation.
- If you are using the anonymous survey link, you can append it so that everyone who clicks on that specific survey link will see the survey in that specific language. To do this, you will take the survey link and place "&Q_lang=languagecode" on the end of it. You will need to replace 'languagecode' with the offical language code of the language you would like to display. All official language codes can be found online.
- If you would like to see in the results which language the respondent took the survey in, you will need to add an embedded data field into the Survey Flow called "RecipientLanguage". This will place a column in your results showing the language code for each respondent.

❖ Scoring

Administer scored rating instruments or tests to respondents. Assign point values to different answer choices, and then optionally display those scores to respondents while they take the survey.

With the Scoring tool you can assign numeric values to individual answer choices that are then added up to give the respondent a score (Figure 6.10). This feature can be used to make a quiz out of your survey and can also facilitate more complex logic functions. You can assign a numeric score to Multiple Choice, Matrix, and Text Entry question types and then grade the questions.

If you are setting up your survey as a quiz, you can show the respondent their score either after each question in the survey or at the end of the survey (Figure 6-9). The respondent can also be shown whether or not they got the answer correct.

When you download the data, additional columns are provided to show the Sum, Weighted Average, and the Weighted Standard Deviation scores for each respondent.

Figure 6-10 Applying scores to survey responses.

TO USE SCORING:

1. Under the Advanced Options drop-down, select **Scoring**.
2. Assign a Scoring value to answer choices. Scoring is only available for Multiple Choice, Matrix, and Text Entry question types.
   - For Multiple Choice and Matrix questions, click on the grayed-out numeric value to enter a value. This turns on Scoring for that particular choice. The default value is "1".
   - Matrix questions can also be scored ascending or descending by row or column. In addition, the same score can be set for an entire row or column.
   - For Text Entry questions, you can enter text and a score for potential answers. Click the "+" button to add additional answers and numeric scores (like New York City, NYC, N.Y.C., etc.).
3. Decide if you want to use the additional reporting options.
   - **Show End of Survey Summary:** Displays a score summary to the participant at the end of the survey. This includes total score, as well as percent correct.
   - **Show Summary After Every Question:** Displays a score summary to the participant after every question. This includes the total score for that individual question. For multiple questions on the same page, the next page will show multiple post-question summaries on the same page.

Q-TIP

- Turn off the Scoring of a choice by going back to Scoring and clicking on answer choice text of the answer choice that has been scored.
- In most cases, you can also click the answer choice text to Turn On Scoring for that choice.
- Sometimes scoring is also referred to as grading. You can enter **GradePercent** and save it as an embedded data field in the Survey Flow for the received percentage of the potential total score. This is just on an individual respondent level.
- If a question is not one of the supported question types, the message "This question type is not currently supported" will be displayed to you on the Scoring page.
- If you would like to base logic upon Scoring, you will first need to put the scoring category into the Survey Flow as embedded data. If you are in the Grade scoring category, you can add an embedded data called "Grade" to the Survey Flow, then for a question in the survey you can add Display Logic that says "If Embedded Data 'Grade' is equal to a 'certain number', then display." The question will only display then if a certain score is obtained.

Test Survey

The Test Survey feature is a simple way to pump some dummy data into your survey (Figure 6-11). It allows you to test out your survey by seeing if the results come through the way you expected. Test Survey allows you to discover problems and make changes to the survey, as needed, before distributing the survey to your actual participants.

Figure 6-11 *Test Survey window.*

TO USE THE TEST SURVEY FEATURE:

1. Select **Test Survey** under the Advanced Options drop-down.
2. Enter the number of test responses you want in the **Test Iterations** text field. The default is "5".
3. Determine if you want to use the additional options (optional).
   - **ALLOW UNANSWERED QUESTIONS:** If selected, some questions might not receive a response. This is to simulate actual respondents who might not answer every question due to skipping the question or skip/display logic.
   - **SHOW VERBOSE OUTPUT:** This means additional information will be provided in the window above the options for each response entered.
   - **ADDITIONAL URL PARAMETERS:** This allows you to include embedded data fields with your responses. Information is entered in the following format: [field name]=[value].
     Example: State=CA

Import Survey

The Qualtrics team has worked very hard to make it so the Edit Survey tab is so easy to use you don't need to import surveys. If you have a survey that you are trying to bring over from another survey software program, it is usually fastest to rebuild the survey in Qualtrics by adding in the questions and pasting in your question text.

However, sometimes importing survey text is necessary. The Import Survey feature allows you to select a file on your machine and import that into the Qualtrics Survey Research Suite.

The text import method is a useful way to get the majority of a survey into the tool. Since not everything available within the tool is available as a formatting option with text files, odds are you will still want to do some formatting or adjusting to the survey after the import.

THERE ARE TWO RECOGNIZED FILE FORMATS FOR IMPORTING FILES INTO THE RESEARCH SUITE:

1) **QUALTRICS SURVEY FORMAT (.QSF):** This format is available only when you export the survey from the Qualtrics Survey tool. You may be working with this file type if another Qualtrics user has exported their survey as a .qsf and given it to you to upload.

2) **TEXT FILE (.TXT):** This is a plain-text export that you might have generated from exporting your survey from another survey software program. Also, if your survey is not in a .qsf format, this is the only other acceptable file format for importing your survey questions.

Figure 6-12 Import Survey dialog window when importing a .qsf file.

TO IMPORT THE QUALTRICS SURVEY FORMAT (.QSF):

1. The .qsf format is only available when you export the survey from the tool (see the Export Survey section below).
2. Under Advanced Options, select **Import Survey**.
3. Click **Browse** (or **Choose File**) and find the .qsf file on your machine.
4. Click **Import**.

When you select your file, a message will display saying, "This import will replace your entire survey and remove all responses." This means if there are any existing questions in the survey already, they will be overwritten. This will also affect any existing data, so make sure you are importing into the correct survey.

IMPORTING A TEXT FILE (.TXT)

This format is best created in a text editor, like Notepad or a similar application. Word processors, like MS Word, can be used, but usually a text editor will function better.

There is a Simple Format and an Advanced Format option. The Simple Format is the easier, less specific format. The Advanced Format is more specific and provides more control, but it is also more complicated to set up.

INSTRUCTIONS FOR SIMPLE FORMAT:

The text file option is appropriate in an automated system, where you have a back-end program that automatically generates .TXT surveys for you to import. To create a survey in the Simple .TXT format,

1. Format questions.
   - A question begins with a number followed by a period ("."). Choices are below the question text with a blank line between the question and the answer choices.
   - For Matrix questions: Answers are after choices with a blank line between.
   - Make a question multiple answer by using **[[MultipleAnswer]]** on the line just below the question text.
   - Insert a page break by entering **[[PageBreak]]**.
2. Save as a .TXT file and import into Qualtrics.

HERE IS AN EXAMPLE OF A .TXT FILE FOR THE SIMPLE FORMAT:

1. This is a multiple choice question. Every question starts with a number followed by a period. There should be a blank line between the question text and the choices.

   a   b   c   d

[[Block:My Block Name]]
2. This is a multiple choice multiple answer question.

   [[MultipleAnswer]]
   a   b   c   d

[[PageBreak]]
3. This is a matrix question that has question text on multiple lines. As long as the text is no more than one line below, it continues to be part of the question text.
   It is a matrix question because it has two groups of choices.
   Row a   Row b   Row c

   Scale 1   Scale 2   Scale 3

4. This is a matrix multiple answer question.

[[MultipleAnswer]]
Row a   Row b   Row c

Scale 1   Scale 2   Scale 3

[[Block]]
5. What is your gender?

Male   Female

Instructions for Advanced Formating:

1. Format questions.
   - The file must begin with the [[AdvancedFormat]] tag.
   - A question begins with the [[Question:]] tag, with the user type code appearing after the colon.
   - Available question types: MC, Matrix, TE, CS, RO, DB.
       - MC = Multiple Choice
       - Matrix = Matrix Table
       - TE = Text Entry
       - CS = Constant Sum
       - RO = Rank Order
       - DB = Text/Graphic (Descriptive Block)
   - Choices start with the [[Choices]] tag and are one per line afterward.
   - Answers start with [[Answers]] tag and are one per line below it.
   - Make question multiple answer using [[MultipleAnswer]].
   - Use [[ID:#]] to set the id of the question (shown as the export tag). Replace "#" with the numeric value.
   - Insert a page break using [[PageBreak]].
   - Insert a block with [[Block]] or [[Block:Name Goes Here]] to name the block. Replace "Name Goes Here" with the block name to use.
2. Save as a .txt file and import into the Qualtrics Survey Research Suite.

HERE IS AN EXAMPLE OF A .TXT FILE FOR THE ADVANCED FORMAT:

[[AdvancedFormat]]

[[Question:MC]]
[[ID:q1]]
This is a multiple choice question.

    [[Choices]]
         a   b   c   d

[[Question:MC:MultipleAnswer]]

[[ID:q2]]
This is a multiple choice question multiple answer question.

[[Choices]]
a   b   c   d

[[PageBreak]]

[[Question:Matrix]]
This question is a matrix question.

It has text on multiple lines.
[[Choices]]
Row a   Row b   Row c

[[Answers]]
Scale 1   Scale 2   Scale 3

[[Question:Matrix]]
[[MultipleAnswer]]
This question is a matrix multiple answer question. Use the HTML break tag to actually have question text recognized as different lines.

It has lots of question text on multiple lines.

[[Choices]]
a   b   c

[[Answers]]
1   2   3

✳ Export Survey

Export a copy of the survey (.qsf) or export it to Word for storage or printing.

Exporting your survey is useful for keeping your own backup of the survey outside of the Qualtrics Survey Research Suite. You can export your survey into the Qualtrics Survey Format (.qsf). This is an .xml file of your survey. You can also use this as a method for sending someone a copy of your survey, though you can use the Copy button on the My Surveys page to copy it directly into their account as well.

EXPORTING YOUR SURVEY TO .QSF FORMAT:
Under Advanced Options, click **Export Survey**. A .qsf file will download to your machine.

EXPORT SURVEY TO WORD

The Export Survey to Word feature provides you with a .docx file compatible with Microsoft Word (Figure 6-13). This is useful for printing out paper surveys, as well as for collaboration, as you can email the file to clients to look at the survey with you. Also, because this document shows you how each answer choice is coding, downloading it can provide you with a key as you analyze your data.

Since it is a document, it can be edited as needed. Of course, any changes you make in the document will also need to be made within the tool so the survey is up to date.

Figure 6-13 Available options when exporting survey to Word.

TO EXPORT YOUR SURVEY TO MICROSOFT WORD:
1. Under Advanced Options, select **Export Survey to Word**.
2. Choose which options you would like to use. All three options are selected by default.
   - **Number Questions with Export Tags**: Determines whether question numbers are displayed. The numbers are the Export Tags, which are the numbers appearing at the top left corner of each question.
   - **Show Logic**: Allows Skip Logic and Display Logic to be represented in the downloaded file. Branch Logic in the Survey Flow will not be shown.
   - **Show Coded Values**: This shows the numeric value of each answer choice. If Recode Values has been used, then the recoded answer choice value will be displayed.
3. Click **Export**.

Summary

This chapter completes the two sections in the book on how to build a great survey in Qualtrics. You will have noticed that in this chapter we covered complex features that you will use only for special cases. However, even if you are not going to be integrating with Salesforce or translating your survey into multiple languages, its important to know that these options are available.

If you do find that you are going to use one of these special features, we hope that you have found the guidelines in this chapter useful as you implement them. After reading this chapter, you should have a clear idea of how to use Triggers, integrate with your Salesforce account, set up a Conjoint Analysis, Translate your survey, set up Scoring and Import and Export.

In the next section of the book, you will learn everything you need to know about how to distribute your survey to respondents and analyze data through View Results. Good luck and feel free to revisit these building chapters whenever it's time to create a new survey. You never know what you might learn.

Chapter 7

Distribute Survey

Building the perfect survey is useless if you don't distribute it.
Find out all your distribution options here.

IN THIS CHAPTER YOU WILL LEARN HOW TO:

- Prepare a Survey Link
- Email a Survey to a Panel
- Access the Email History
- Distribute through Social Media
- Use the In-page Pop-up and Website Feedback options
- Use the Survey Director

Distribute Survey Tab

The *Distribute Survey* tab contains all the options you need to distribute your survey. There are seven options you can choose from as you decide how you would like to collect data. Although you will most likely be using the anonymous
survey link or the Email Survey options, it is good to become familiar with all of your distribution options.

If this is your first time going to the *Distribute Survey* tab for the selected survey, you will need to first Activate your survey. Click the **Activate your survey to collect responses** link. This is the equivalent of clicking the checkbox on the My Surveys page to activate the survey.

The following sections contain details about each distribution method. As you read each section, take time to explore these options within your account. Click on the anonymous survey link to see what happens. Send a test distribution to yourself. Become familiar with these options before you start collecting responses.

SURVEY LINK

The basic survey link. Responses on this link are anonymous.

This is the easiest way to distribute your survey. You can copy/paste the survey link into an email or onto your website or blog.

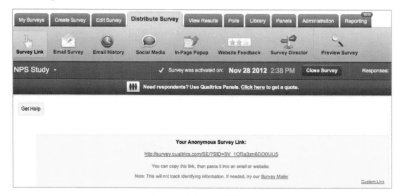

Figure 7-1 *Survey Link page.*

This is an Anonymous Survey Link. Each participant uses the same link, so the Qualtrics Survey Research Suite doesn't keep track of, or know who, takes each survey. If you want to track respondents and identify who responded to which survey, use the Email Survey option. Traits of the Anonymous Survey Link:

- Any responses collected through this link will be anonymous (No panel information is attached to the response).
- Saves the respondent's progress through cookies. If the respondent starts the survey, leaves, and comes back to the same browser, they will start where they left off.
- There is no limit to how many times this link can be used. Respondents can pass it on to other respondents to take.

If you would like to prevent individuals from taking the survey multiple times through the anonymous survey link, you will want to enable Prevent Ballot Box Stuffing under Survey Options. This will put a cookie on the respondent's browser, preventing them from taking the survey twice.

EMAIL SURVEY

Clicking on the Email Survey icon presents an email form that allows you to conduct a mail merge and send a unique email and unique survey link to a list of people. This is probably the most common way to distribute your survey.

Customize your survey invitation and track responses from each member of a panel. Sends a unique email and unique link to each potential respondent.

Figure 7-2 *Email Survey Page.*

Traits of the Unique Link:

- By default, each unique link can only be used once, which prevents spamming.
- The data collected through the link is automatically attached to the respondents' panel information.
- The link allows you to track responses in progress and send out reminder and thank you messages to your contacts.
- The link automatically saves the respondents' data as they progress through the survey.

TO DISTRIBUTE THE SURVEY THROUGH EMAIL SURVEY:

1. In the "To" area, select who you want to send the survey to.
   - Click **Enter Email Address** to paste in the list information. You can paste multiple rows and columns at the same time and Qualtrics will recognize those distinctions. Using this option automatically saves a panel with a date and time stamp as the panel's name.
   - Hover over **My Library** (or a **Group Library**) to find and select a panel, a sample from a panel, or an individual within a panel. For information on importing a panel, see Chapter 8: Panels.
2. In the "When" area, select the time you want to send out the survey. Under **Custom**, you can specify the exact date and time you want the survey to be sent out. Your options are to:
   - Send Now
   - Send in 1 or 8 hours
   - Send in 1, 3, 7, 14, 28 days
   - Custom: Select the date and time you want it to go out. Specify the time according to your time zone.
3. If necessary, adjust the "From Name" and "Reply-To Email Address." These are automatically populated from the information set in your user account.
4. Enter a "Subject" line for your email.
5. Enter your email message. Enter the message directly into the Rich Content Editor field. After editing, you will need to save your message by clicking the **Save** or **Save As** button.
   - If needed, click **Load a Saved Message** to select an existing message. This can be a message you used on a previous mailing, or a message created in your Message Library. You can edit saved messages. If you make changes, you will be prompted to click the **Save** button to the right side.
6. If necessary, click the **Advanced Options** button to set or modify the behavior of your mailing and survey link.

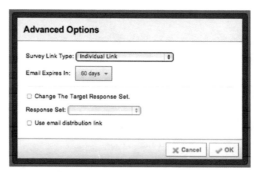

Figure 7-3 Advanced Email Options.

ADVANCED OPTIONS:
- **SURVEY LINK TYPE:** The survey link can carry with it certain constraints related to respondent link sharing and respondent identification (single use, multiple use, and anonymous).
  - **INDIVIDUAL LINK:** The default selection. This is a unique link for each member of the panel you send to. It can only be used once. The Reminder and Thank You options on the Email History page will not be available with the individual link.
  - **MULTIPLE COMPLETES PER LINK:** This option is designed to obtain a "snowball"

type sample, where people forward the survey link to others who might be qualified or interested in taking the same survey. When the response comes in it will be associated with the person who was originally sent the link through the panel.

- **ANONYMOUS LINK:** This is the same link as the link found on the Survey Link page. Those who take the survey through this link are considered anonymous within the results. The Reminder and Thank You options on the Email History page will not be available when using the anonymous link.

- **EMAIL EXPIRES IN:** The amount of time until the link expires. Once the link is clicked, this expiration date no longer applies. By default, the link expires in 60 days. The options are from 1-90 days. Alternatively, you can click Custom to specify an exact date and time when the link will expire.

- **CHANGE THE TARGET RESPONSE SET:** This allows you to change the response set responses from this distribution are saved in. If you select the option, you can change the Response Set using the drop-down. You can create new Response Sets under Survey Options on the *Edit Survey* tab. Most people will not need to use this option, so it is not recommended unless you specifically want to place your data from this panel in a different place than the rest of the survey data.

- **USE EMAIL DISTRIBUTION LINK:** This option is useful when you would like to generate unique links but do not want to send them out through our mailer. For this option, check the box for **Use email distribution link** and select **Don't send emails**. If you select this option and Schedule Mailing, no messages will be sent to participants. Instead, in the Email History section, you'll be able to click the **Actions** drop-down next to your mailing and select **Download Mailing History** to get a list of survey links. You can then send these links out through a Mail Merge in your own email account.

- **DON'T SEND EMAILS (FOR MANUAL GENERATION OF SURVEY LINKS):** This option is only available if you select **Use email distribution link**. This is useful if you need to get the unique links for sending through your own email server. You can download the links from the Email History page.

  When using this option, you will need to create a panel, but the panel does not need to contain real email addresses. You can put in devnull@qemailserver.com, but still put in the real name of the respondents. When the links are generated, the names will be linked to the survey link but no emails will be sent out.

7. Click **Schedule Mailing**. This button will say **Send Now** if you select the Send Now option in the "When" area.

Send Test Email allows you to send an email to yourself with your current settings in place without having to schedule the entire mailing. This way you can make sure everything is coming through correctly. This feature is **optional**. Also, the link that is sent to you through Send Test Email will be an anonymous link.

EMAIL HISTORY

Schedule Reminder and Thank You messages to the mailings scheduled on the Email Survey page. You will also find basic tracking of all the mailings you have done for the survey.

The Email History page is directly linked to the Email Survey page. When you schedule a mailing, you are automatically directed to the Email History page. On this page you are able to see the basic information of your mailing as well as take further actions with it (Figure 7-4).

Status	Recipient	Subject	Date	Emails Failed	Surveys Started	Surveys Finished	Actions
○	Mailing List	Feedback survey - your opinion is important!	16 Jun 2011 3:33 PM 51m left	0/0	0	0	▼

Figure 7-4 Email History table.

There are eight columns of information contained in the Email History table. The **Actions** column is a menu of options.

- **STATUS:** This refers to the various dots at the bottom of the page, which signify different statuses.
    - **CLEAR:** The mailing is scheduled to be sent.
    - **ORANGE:** The emails are currently being sent.
    - **GREEN:** The mailing was successfully sent.
    - **RED:** There was an error and no emails were sent.
- **RECIPIENT:** The name of the panel you are sending to.
- **SUBJECT:** The subject line you entered when you scheduled the mailing.
- **DATE:** The date and time the mailing is scheduled to be sent. If the mailing has already been sent, this column shows the time it was distributed. The time is set to your time zone.
- **EMAILS FAILED:** Shows a count of total emails that were unable to be sent. The left value is the value of emails failed, while the right value is the total of emails in the panel (emails failed / total emails in panel).
    - This will not show the number of bounce backs. It will just show a count of emails that the mailer was literally unable to send. To see the specific emails, select Download Mailing History under the Actions dropdown.
- **SURVEYS STARTED:** The number of surveys that were started from this specific distribution.
- **SURVEYS FINISHED:** Count of the surveys from this panel that have been completed. This will not include partially completed responses.
- **ACTIONS:** A menu of additional options.
    - **EDIT DISTRIBUTION:** Select this option to edit the mailing and its settings before it is sent out. If the mailing has already been sent, selecting this option will show the mailing's settings as they were when the mailing was sent.
    - **DOWNLOAD MAILING HISTORY:** This downloads a .csv (comma separated values) file to be opened in Excel. It contains each panel member's basic panel information (name and email), as well as their status, survey link, and response ID (if they completed the survey).
    - **SEND REMINDER OR THANK YOU:** Choose to remind panel members to take the survey, or thank those who did take the survey for their diligence! See the following section for more information on scheduling Reminder and Thank You messages.
    - **DELETE DISTRIBUTION:** Removes the record of the distribution from the Email History page. If the mailing has not gone out yet, it cancels it. If Qualtrics is in the middle of sending to a large panel, deleting the distribution will not cancel it. Also, if the mailing is already sent, this will not do anything to the distribution

- Deleting the distribution is not recommended, especially if you've sent to it already. Once the distribution is removed, you can no longer schedule Reminder and Thank You messages.

SEND REMINDER OR THANK YOU

The tool will smartly send a Reminder or Thank You message depending on who has or has not taken the survey.

Scheduling a Reminder or Thank You message is very similar to scheduling the initial invite mailing. Each option looks at the panel members and sends according to those who match certain criteria.

CRITERIA FOR REMINDER AND THANK YOU:
- **REMINDER:** Only sends to those who have not completed the survey. Those who started the survey but didn't finish, as well as those who never started the survey, will receive the Reminder.
    - Scheduled Reminders place a bell icon in the Recipient field of the Email History.
- **THANK YOU:** Only sends to those who completed the survey. It will not send to partial completes or those who did not start the survey.
    - Scheduled Thank You messages place a post-it note icon in the Recipient field.

SCHEDULING A REMINDER OR THANK YOU:
1. On the **Email History** page, click the **Actions** button and click on **Send Reminder or Thank You**.
2. At the top of the message wizard, select whether you want to schedule a Reminder or Thank You. See the criteria explanation above for more information.
3. In the **When** area, specify when you want the mailing to go out. This is just like the "When" area of the initial invite mailing.
4. Adjust the **Name**, **Reply-To Email**, and **Subject** fields. These fields are automatically populated by what was used when the initial mailing was scheduled.
5. Enter or select **message text** appropriate for the message you're scheduling.
    - Just like the initial invite mailing, you can enter a message here, or select one under the **Load a Saved Message** menu. You will be prompted to save any changes you make to a message.
    - For the **Thank You**, you can delete the default text ("Follow this link to the survey"), as you do not need to pipe in a survey link or opt-out link.
6. When ready, click the **Send** button to schedule your Reminder or Thank You.

💬 SOCIAL MEDIA

Ever thought about linking up to your favorite social networks to distribute your survey?

The Social Media page provides an easy way for you to place your anonymous survey link into your social media networks. The Research Suite integrates with a rather extensive list of social networks. You can even grab a QR (Quick Response) Code for smartphone users.

Figure 7-5 Social Media button.

SOCIAL NETWORKS

The Qualtrics Survey Research Suite currently integrates with the following social networks:

- Twitter
- Facebook
- LinkedIn
- Blogger
- Buzz
- Digg
- StumbleUpon
- Reddit
- Delicious
- MySpace
- Orkut

To use the Social Media feature:

1. Select the social network with which to integrate.
2. Enter an HTML Title. This is the name of the link that appears at the top of the browser tab. This would be something like "Product X Feedback Survey." Each service will use this slightly differently.
3. Enter the Meta Description. This is to describe the content of the link. For example, in Facebook, it's the light gray description appearing below the title of the video link someone posts. Each service has slight differences.
4. Click the **Save and Continue** button.
5. A window will open prompting you for the username and password credentials of the selected social media network.

Each social network service has slight differences in their HTML Title and Meta Description fields. It is a good idea to run a quick test beforehand to see how it is used on the selected network.

SMARTPHONE QR CODE

Get a QR Code image specific to your survey. People can scan your QR Code with their smartphone and get directly to your survey.

QR Codes are becoming more and more common with smartphones. Similar to a barcode, the provided QR code is a code of your survey URL. The phone can scan the QR code and be automatically directed to your survey.

To use the Smartphone QR Code:

1. On the Social Media page, right click the **Smartphone QR Code**.
2. In the menu, select the option to **Save the image**.
3. Place the QR Code where smartphone users will be able to find it.

Figure 7-6 Sample QR Code.

IN-PAGE POPUP

The In-Page Popup is a less-intrusive version of the traditional popup. It is called an "in-page popup" because it is actually a part of your webpage, rather than a separate window. It will not be blocked by pop-up blockers.

Have a window scroll across your website inviting site visitors to take your survey.

Figure 7-7 In-Page Popup button.

TO USE THE IN-PAGE POPUP:
1) Go to the *Distribute Survey* tab and click the **In-Page Popup** button.
   - If you've never been to this page before, click the **Preview Popup** button at the bottom to see it in action.
2) Adjust the Popup Text as needed. The default is "Please take a moment to participate in a survey."
3) Adjust the Link Text as needed. This text will appear in the popup as a hyperlink. The default is "Click here."
4) It is recommended that you click the **More Options** button to take advantage of the additional options and further customize your pop-up.
   - **DISPLAY RATE:** This is how frequently the Pop-up displays itself to your site visitors. The default is 100%. Adjust the slider to change this.
   - **DISPLAY AFTER:** Once the page finishes loading, this is the amount of time before the pop-up displays. Drag the slider to adjust the time. Sometimes users only want to display the pop-up to those who spend more time on their site (e.g., 30 seconds as opposed to 3 seconds).
   - **PREVENT REPEATED DISPLAY:** Similar to Prevent Ballot-Box Stuffing, this uses a browser-based cookie to remember if the pop-up has been presented to someone already. This way you don't have to present the pop-up to your visitors every time they visit.
   - **ANIMATE:** Determines how the pop-up displays to the respondent. The default is to have the pop-up scroll in from the middle-left. You can have it scroll in from other locations, or not scroll in from anywhere. Here are your animation options:
     - Top-Left
     - Top-Center
     - Top-Right
     - Middle-Left
     - Middle-Right
     - Bottom-Left
     - Bottom-Center
     - Bottom-Right

- **POPUP WIDTH AND POPUP HEIGHT:** Adjust the size of the pop-up window scrolling across the screen. The default is 400x300 (width x height).
- **SURVEY WIDTH AND SURVEY HEIGHT:** Adjust the size of the survey window when someone clicks the pop-up link. The default is 900x600 (width x height).

5) After changes are made, click **Preview Pop-up** and test out your survey to make sure it displays correctly.

6) When ready, click **Add Pop-up to My Website** to get the JavaScript for the pop-up. Use this code to place the pop-up on your website or blog, or send it to your IT department to have them place it on your organization's site.

The In-Page Pop-up will not remember your pop-up settings after you leave the page. If you want to keep track of the code, paste the code into a text editor, like Notepad, and save it to your computer.

⭐⭐ WEBSITE FEEDBACK

The Website Feedback option allows you to place a feedback button/link on your website, similar to what you see on banking and credit card sites. When the respondent clicks on the button/link, your survey will pop-up.

In the top-right corner of the Feedback page, there is a preview of what your feedback button will look like on the page.

Figure 7-8 *Website Feedback button.*

TO USE THE WEBSITE FEEDBACK BUTTON:

1. Choose how you would like your link to appear.
   - White background with yellow stars.
   - Black background with yellow stars.
   - Text link. Enter the text you would like to display.

2. Click **More Options** to see additional options you can use to customize the Website Feedback button.
   - **CURSOR TOOL TIP:** This is the text that displays when you hover your mouse over the feedback graphic or link.
   - **POPUP SIZE WIDTH AND HEIGHT:** This refers to the window that displays containing the survey when you click the feedback button.

3. When ready, click the **Add Feedback Link To My Website** button. This will give you the JavaScript you need to post this link onto your website or blog. You can also send it to your IT department.

SURVEY DIRECTOR

The Survey Director is a very powerful distribution tool. Through a single URL, you can set conditions controlling what is displayed to a visitor and *when*. With some similarities to the Qualtrics Site Intercept product, the Survey Director opens up some of the site intercept functionality to every Research Suite user.

Figure 7-9 *Survey Director button.*

Control the experience for your website visitors by controlling how, when and what they see. Dynamically link to different surveys, polls, reports, or other web pages depending on the logic you set.

With the Survey Director, you can post one link on your website or in an email, and then choose what that link will do. For instance, you could have the link point to a survey from Monday through Wednesday, and then point to a public report of the survey results from Thursday through Sunday.

For a high traffic website, place a single link on your website and then have the link direct your visitors to a different survey (about different products or departments) for each day of the week (Figure 7-10). Then you could also display a public report for each survey once it is finished collecting data.

TO USE SURVEY DIRECTOR:
1. On the *Distribute Survey* tab, click the **Survey Director** button.
2. Click the **Create New Director** button to start. This automatically adds an Action Set to your Director. The Action Set is the beef of the Survey Director. This is where you specify your logic and what you want to display. You can add as many Action Sets as you need.
3. Give your Survey Director a name (field at top-left).
4. Click **Add Conditional Statement** to set logic controlling when the item below will be displayed. If you are using the Survey Director, odds are you want some logic in place, but this certainly isn't a requirement. You can base logic on the following items:
    - **DATE:** You can check to see if the Date Is, Is Not, Is Before, Is After, Is or Is Before, Is or Is After, a specified date (YYYY-MM-DD).
    - **DAY:** This allows you to check if the current day Is or Is Not the specified day of the week.
    - **TIME:** This allows you to check to see if the current time Is Before or Is After a specified time. Time is specified in 24-hour format (HH:MM).
    - **STATUS:** Check to see if a Survey or Poll is active or not active before showing an item.
    - **QUOTA:** Check a quota and see if the quota's value has been met, if it's equal to a particular value or if it is greater than or less than a particular value.
5. Choose what to Link to. The options you can link to are the following:

- **SURVEY:** Choose a survey in your account and have the Survey Director link to it.
- **POLL:** Choose a poll in your account and have the Survey Director link to it.
- **PUBLIC REPORT:** Choose a public report from one of your surveys and link to it. You will need to set up a public report in the View Results section in order to use this.
    - This is typically used to show your results after you've finished collecting the survey data. It is a good idea to use it in conjunction with a specific date and time. When you do this, you don't have to manually make any changes later. The Survey Director will take care of it for you.
- **USER DEFINED URL:** Redirect to any URL you choose. This is another useful option when you finish collecting data or if someone doesn't match the criteria to take the survey.

6. If necessary, use the **Click Here To Add Action Set** button to add an additional Action Set. This makes it possible to address the situation where someone doesn't match the previously specified condition(s).
    - Repeat steps 4 and 5 above as needed on any additional Action Sets.
7. When finished with the setup, click the **Click here to generate link button** at the top of the Survey Director. This gives you one URL that checks the logic across all Action Sets within the Director.

Q-TIP

- Assign Embedded Data to those matching the criteria of a particular Action Set:
    1. Click the **Embedded Data** button at the bottom right corner.
    2. Click **Add Embedded Data**.
    3. Enter an embedded data field name in the **Name** text field on the left.
    4. Enter a value for the field in the **Value** text field to the right.
    5. Use the "**+**" button to the right to add additional embedded data fields.
    6. Click **Save** to save your embedded data assignments.
- You can also add additional Action Sets by hovering your mouse over an existing Action set and clicking the green "+" button at the top right or bottom right.
- Remove an existing Action Set by hovering your mouse over the Action Set and clicking the red "-" button to the right.

Summary

There are many great options to choose from when you are ready to distribute your survey. If you would like to make your survey available to a large undefined sample or collect data through a "snowball" method, you can distribute your survey by posting the anonymous survey link on the Internet. The other popular distribution method is to send the survey to a predefined panel through the Qualtrics Mailer. You can carry this out by going to Email Survey and setting up the distribution. The following chapter, Chapter 8, will tell you everything you need to know about building a panel to use with the Qualtrics mailer.

Qualtrics also provides a group of tools that make it easy for you to post your link on webpages and social media sites. Our Social Media, In-page Pop-up, Website Feedback, and Survey Director tools will help you get your survey noticed and aid you in collecting all the data you need to carry out your research.

After you collect your data, you will want to view and analyze your data through the View Results tab. Information on the View Results tab, including how to view reports and download data, can be found in Chapter 9: View Results.

Chapter 8

Panels

Building and maintaining a panel is all the rage. Check out the latest features that Qualtrics has for companies that create in-house panels.

IN THIS CHAPTER WE WILL ANSWER THE QUESTIONS:

- What is a panel?
- How do I create a panel?
- How do I manage my panels?
- How do I create a panel sample?

A panel is a mailing list you can create in Qualtrics through importing the contact information of your respondents. A panel can include the recipient name, email address, and any additional information (Embedded Data) you would like stored with the panel members' responses.

The *Panels* tab is where your mailing lists are stored. The *Panels* tab is basically a library for your panels. In fact, you can have a Panel Library for a group (your company, department, or work group) so users can share panels. If you have access to multiple Groups or Libraries, just click the **Current Panel Library** button to select a different library.

The Panels Tab

The *Panels* tab is like the My Surveys tab in that several functions can be performed within it. First, it is where you can create panels (Figure 8-1). After you create some panels, you can see that each panel has associated Panel Actions icons (Figure 8-2) next to them in the Panel Actions column.

From the Panel Members page, you can click a panel's name to view and edit information about a member of the panel.

The Sample Management tab allows you to filter a panel down to a subgroup of contacts.

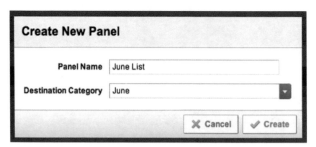

Figure 8-1 Create New Panel window.

To create a new panel:
1. On the *Panels* tab, make sure you're on the Panels page, then click the **Create New Panel** button.
2. Provide a name for your panel in the Panel Name text field.

3. Specify a Destination Category (like a folder) for your panel. This is optional. If you do not provide a category, it will be placed into the "Unassigned" category.
   • If you would like to create a new category, type into the text field.
   • Select an existing category by clicking the blue drop-down arrow.
4. Click **Create**. This will automatically jump you to the Panel Members page.

Figure 8-2 Panel Action Items.

ADD PANEL MEMBERS

Adding panel members is a quick and easy way to copy and paste your list of contacts into the tool. It can be quite useful for shorter lists of panel members.

This option can be useful for small lists, but for larger lists you will probably want to use the import feature.

Build your own panel. Once you create a panel you need to place people in it.

To paste in a list of panel members:
1. First click on your panel from your panel list to have it open in the Panel Members section.
2. Click the **Add Panel Members** button.
3. In the Panel field, make sure the correct panel is selected. It will preselect whichever panel you chose to select to the Panel Members page in the first place.
4. Click the "**+**" button on the right side to add any additional columns. The first two will be optional panel fields that are less commonly used (External Data Reference, Language). All fields after will be in the form of Embedded Data.
   • Click the column header to edit it, if needed.
5. Paste in your list.

Q-TIP

• Remember, you can copy your entire spreadsheet (all of your rows and columns) and paste it in all at once. The tool will be smart and recognize the different rows and columns. Just make sure your spreadsheet's columns are in the same order as what you specified when pasting. It will always start with Email, First Name, Last Name, External Data Reference, and Language. Leave blank any columns you don't use.
• Remember not to paste in your column headers from your spreadsheet. Those are taken care of in the headers of the Add Panel Members dialog.
• The Add Panel Members option is actually the same as pasting in your panel on the Email Survey page when you select Enter Email Addresses in the **To** field.

• Make sure there is no white space before or after the email addresses. White space will invalidate the email addresses.

PANEL ACTIONS

Once your panel is created, you will see it listed in the Panels section. Next to each panel in your Panels section under **Panel Actions** is a list of actions that can be taken with your panel. The following is a detailed explanation of each.

EXPORT PANEL

Export Panel allows you to export your panel as a .csv, .xml, or .html file.

To export a panel:
1. On the Panels page, click the Export Panel button for the panel you want.
2. Choose a Format for the file. There are three options:
   • **CSV:** Exports a .csv file that is typically opened in Excel. CSV stands for Comma Separated Values.
   • **XML:** Exports a .xml file. This file type is typically used when importing to database applications. XML stands for eXtensible Markup Language.
   • **HTML:** Exports an html file that is typically viewed in a web browser. The data is placed into an HTML based table. HTML stands for HyperText Markup Language.
3. Choose if you want to Export Embedded Data.
   • **Yes** will download all embedded data.
   • **No** doesn't include any embedded data fields in the download.
   • **Only Specified Items** expands the dialog window to include a text field for entering the field names of the specific embedded data fields you want to export.
4. Choose a Subscription Status. This is referring to whether or not your panel members have opted out of receiving any more mailings.
   • *All* includes everyone in the panel, regardless of Subscription Status.
   • *Subscribed* only includes those who have not clicked the opt-out link in the mailings you have sent them.
   • *Unsubscribed* only includes those who have clicked the opt-out link in the mailings you have sent them.
5. Click the **Export** button.

EMBEDDED DATA

The Embedded Data option loads a list for all embedded data fields and their associated values used in the panel. This can be a useful reference to make sure embedded data fields and values were imported correctly. If someone was not imported correctly, it will appear as a separate field or value within the list.

MOVE PANEL

Selecting Move Panel will allow you to move the panel to a different library.

To move a panel:
1. On the Panels page of the *Panels* tab, click the Move Panel button for the panel you want to move.
2. Under Destination Panel Library, select a library where you want the panel to be.
3. Specify a Destination Category (like a folder) for your panel. This is optional. If you do not provide a category,
   it will be placed in the "Unassigned" category.
   - Create a new category by clicking into the text field and typing in a category.
   - Select an existing category by clicking the blue arrow.
4. Edit the Panel Name, if needed.
5. Click **Move**.

SEND EMAIL

You can send a non-survey-invite email to your panel members. Typically this gets used to notify panel members of forthcoming survey invites.

Send Email allows you to send a pre-notification or other email to your panel. A separate email is sent to each panel member. This is separate from sending an email invitation and should not be used as such. See the explanation below for more information.

To send an email to your panel that does not include a survey link:
1. On the Panels page of the *Panels* tab, click the **Send Email** button next to the panel you want to email.
2. Specify a From Name and Reply-To Email for the email to come from.
3. Enter a Subject for the email.
4. Enter the email message text and use the Rich Content Editor for formatting.
5. Click **Send** when you are ready to email your panel members. Your panel members will each be sent a separate email.

ALERT: The Send Email option will **not** keep a record of the mailing. It is not like sending an email invite on the Email Survey page and is not to be used for that purpose. The Send Email may be useful for a pre-notification or other communication to an ongoing panel you have organized. If you want to send out a survey invitation with a link to the survey, go to the *Distribute Survey* tab.

With Send Email, you can use the piped text icon ({a}) to personalize the message with a name or other information
(like embedded data).

ᵢᵢᵢ PANEL MEMBERS

The Panel Members page is where you get to see the details of your panel members (Figure 8-3). You can view their individual panel and embedded data information. This is the same page where you can import and update a list of panel members.

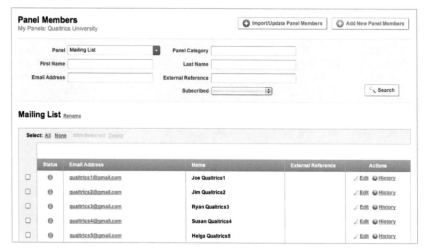

Figure 8-3 Panel Members page.

All instructions in the Panel Members area are based on a panel being created already. If you need to create a panel, see the bottom of page 148 for details on how to create a panel.

IMPORT FROM A FILE

Upload a spreadsheet of panel members from your computer.

Importing from a file (.csv) is the most common and the quickest panel importing method (Figure 8-4).

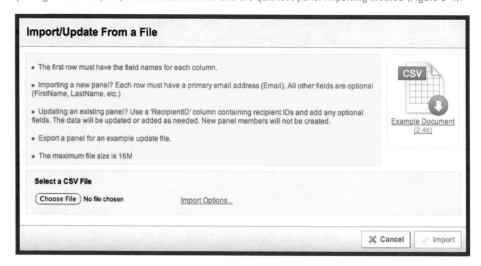

Figure 8-4 Import From a File dialog.

To import a panel:

1. Go to the Panel Members page of the *Panels* tab and click the **Import From a File** button.
   - If you already have panel members in the panel, then click **Import/Update Panel Members** near the top of the page.
     - a) Under **Import to Panel**, select a panel to import your list into. This will be selected already if you clicked on a panel on the Panels page or just created a new panel.
     - b) **Click Import/Update From a File**.
     - c) Continue to follow the directions below.
2. Click **Browse or Choose File** and select the .csv file on your computer.
     - a) If your file isn't already saved as a .csv, you will need to save it as a .csv. To do this, go to **File** in the Excel toolbar and select **Save As**. Choose the file type as CSV (Comma Delimited).
3. Once you have selected the file, a preview of the first five rows of your spreadsheet will display.
4. Make sure the columns of your spreadsheet are being correctly interpreted.
   - If the columns are not displaying correctly, click **Import Options** and work with the options. See the associated Q-tip area for more information.
   - If the column headers are incorrect, click the menu at the top of each column and select the correct heading. This is especially important for the panel fields (FirstName, LastName, and Email).
5. Click **Import**.

Q - T I P

- Depending on if you are using Windows or Mac OS X, Excel will call a .csv file something slightly different.
  - Windows: CSV (Comma Delimited)
  - Mac OS X: Comma Separated Values (.csv)
- Some other spreadsheet applications will call a .csv file "Text CSV (.csv)".
- Since a .csv file is really just a text file, make sure all your data is on the same tab in the spreadsheet. A text file can't handle the same formatting as a regular spreadsheet file type.
- If your spreadsheet is not interpreted correctly and is all jumbled together in the preview, click **Import Options**. Try using a different Delimiter and/or Enclosure. Each time you make a different selection, the preview will reload to see if it is now loading correctly.
  - In some regions outside North America, Excel is set to use a non-comma delimiter when saving a .csv file. The system should recognize this, but if not, try using the Import Options.

UPDATE PANEL MEMBERS

As you collect information on your panel members, you might want to reference that information in future surveys. Now you can use the update feature.

Edit your panel member information that is already saved.

To update a panel:

The easiest way to do this is to download your existing panel first. Downloading your panel gives you a RecipientID column, which is what is used to determine if the panel member exists for updating or is a new panel member. Download your panels using the Export Panel option on the Panels page.

1. Export the panel. See the Panels section for information on exporting your panel.
2. Make any necessary changes to the panel members. ALERT: Be sure to keep the RecipientID column in your sheet.
3. Save the updated spreadsheet (remember, it needs to be a .csv).
4. Import the list. See the previous instructions on how to import a panel for more information on this.

ALERT: If your file does not contain the RecipientID column, the Qualtrics Survey Research Suite will import the list as completely new panel members. It will not recognize the information as an existing panel member for updating unless they have the RecipientID. If you accidently upload duplicates, you can use the Consolidate Duplicates feature to clean it up, but it is best not to let it happen in the first place.

IMPORT FROM A SURVEY

Let's say you distributed a survey and in that survey you collected contact information from your respondents. With the **Import From a Survey** option, you could take that information and turn it into a panel (Figure 8-5). Import From a Survey lets you create new panel members or update existing panel members.

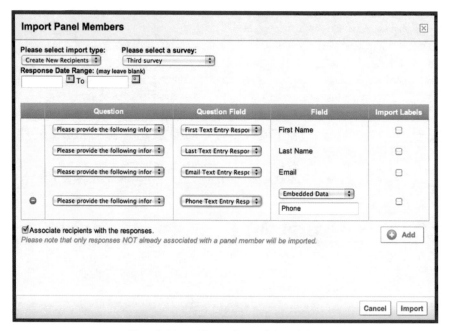

Figure 8-5 Import From a Survey dialog window.

To Import From a Survey:

1. If you have no panels set up, go to the Panel Members page, and select **Import From a Survey**.
2. If you already have a panel set up with panel members, click the **Import/Update Panel Members** button and select **Import/Update From a Survey**.
3. Under **Please select import type**, specify if you want to Update Recipients or Create New Recipients.
4. Under **Please select a survey**, choose the survey containing the information to use in the panel.
5. Under **Response Date Range**, enter a date range of data for the tool to reference. This is optional. If no date is provided, it will look at all data for the survey.
6. In the area below, choose how to populate the panel information.
   a. In the Questions column, select a survey question containing information you would like to pull in.
   b. In the Question Field column, choose a choice or field. On a Text Entry Form question, this is the specific form field (First Name, Last Name).
   c. In the Field column, choose what area of the panel the data should be placed into. This will be Embedded Data, First Name, Last Name, Email, External Data Reference, or Language.
   d. Choose if you want to Import Labels. This refers to standard questions, like a multiple choice question. For example, if it's a yes/no question, the default is to pull in the value (1 or 2), so selecting Import Labels will pull in the actual answer choice text (yes/no).
   e. Click **Add** to pull in additional fields and repeat these 5 (a-e) sub-steps again.
7. When finished, click **Import** to create or update the panel members.

MISCELLANEOUS PANEL MEMBER TASKS

Now that you have panel members in your panel, you can work with the individual panel members and make changes, view their history, or even delete them.

To Edit existing panel members:

1. Select the Panel from the Panels page and in the Panel Members page, click the **Edit** button to the right of the panel member (or click the panel member's email address).
2. In the Edit Panel Member window, you can edit their existing information.
3. Click **Save** when finished.

- **Unsubscribe** allows you to opt panel members out of receiving any more emails from this panel, the same as if they clicked the Opt-Out link in the invite email.
  - Unsubscribed or opted out panel members will display a red dot to the left, as opposed to the green dot.
- **Language** allows you to choose a language for email messages. If the translation is available for the message, it will be sent in that chosen language.
- The **RecipientID** is the ID specific to that panel member. It is the ID mentioned earlier for updating panel members.

To delete existing panel members:

1. On the Panel Members page, click the checkbox to the left of each panel member you want to delete. You can also use the All or None buttons at the top of the panel member list to select all or none of your panel members on the page.
2. Click the red **Delete** button at the top of the list of panel members.

To view panel member history:

1. Click the **History** button to the right of the panel member.
   - The **Email History** table shows the mailings that the respondents have been sent.
   - The **Response History** table shows when they actually responded to surveys.

To search for specific panel members:

1. Enter criteria into search fields at the top of the Panel Members page. The more criteria you enter, the more specific your search will be.
2. Press the **Enter** button to start the search. You can also just press the Enter key on your keyboard.

You can search across multiple panels by removing the panel name in the Panel search field.

SAMPLE MANAGEMENT

Sample Management allows you to filter specific panel segments and distribute your survey to that segment.

The Sample Management area allows you to filter your panel members into smaller groups (Figure 8-6). You can choose to schedule a mailing to a specific sample on the Email Survey page.

Figure 8-6 Sample Management dialog window.

To create a new sample:
1. On the Sample Management page, click the **Create New Sample** button.
2. On the Panel button (top right), choose a panel to pull the sample from. If you were already looking at a panel on the Panel Members page, then that panel will be selected already.
3. In Sample Name, enter a name for your sample.
4. In Max Sample Size, specify the maximum number of panel members for the sample. The Max Sample Size only takes effect if there are more panel members matching the criteria than the Max Sample Size.
   - Click the **Calculator** button for help deciding on your Max Sample Size. You will be prompted to enter your desired number of responses and your expected response rate.
5. Click **Add a Sample Condition** to specify logic for the desired demographic of panel members. If you don't specify a condition, it will just pull a random sample of panel members until it reaches your Max Sample Size, if possible.
6. Choose the type of criteria you would like to use.
   - **EMBEDDED DATA:** Provide a Field Name, whether it's equal to, greater/less than, and the value of the field.
   - **RECIPIENT HISTORY:** Set up a condition based off Last Survey Taken and the Last Email Distribution Date.
   - **RECIPIENT SAMPLE MEMBERSHIP:** Set a condition based off whether the panel members are a Member or Not a Member of another sample of the panel.
7. Click the blue "+" button to the right to add additional logic to your condition. Doing so will allow you to use the And If and Or If logic.
8. When finished, click **Generate Sample** to filter the panel members according to the condition. You can make any edits as needed and click **Refilter Samples** to regenerate your sample.
9. Click **Close** to close out the Create Sample window when finished.

Q-TIP

After your sample has been filtered, you can click the **Edit** button to see the information for the panel members in the sample. You can also click the **History** button to see their panel history, like on the Panel Members page.

Summary

Good data collection is dependent on a good panel. When you distribute your survey to a panel in Qualtrics, all of the panel information is attached to the responses of the panel members taking the survey. From this, you can tell who has taken the survey and track their responses.

Through the Research Suite, it is simple to create your panel and distribute your survey to it. Use the panel upload options available to you to make your contacts accessible in your account.

With the *Panels* tab, you can choose to upload your contacts using a spreadsheet if you are using a large panel, or you can choose to copy and paste your contacts through the "Add New Panel Members" option if you have a smaller distribution. After uploading your panel members, you can go to the Distribute Survey tab and under the Email Survey page, you can select a panel to send your survey to. Once a panel is created, you can distribute any of your surveys to it. It is not connected to any one survey.

In this chapter we also covered the benefits of creating a Panel Sample. If you would like to send the survey to a smaller random sample of your panel, you can do this through Sample Management. You could also specify that you would like to create a sample out of only those respondents who have already taken the survey, those respondents that don't belong to another sample, or respondents that have a specific embedded data value in the panel.

Using these panel features, you will be able to successfully get your survey out to your respondents and collect only the data you want to collect.

Chapter 9

View Results

The View Results tab has many research tools that can help you whip your data into shape. Make your data into a report, analyze it, then share it with your colleagues, all from one location.

The View Results tab is where you go to analyze your data, import or delete responses, and download your data for analysis using external applications. For information on the Qualtrics classic reporting, see Appendix C.

View Reports

"Wow, this is amazing! It's like PowerPoint!" Analyze your data, make it into a report, and share it with your colleagues.

The View Results tab is where you go to analyze your data and build your reports. You can also import or delete responses and download your data for analysis using external applications. For reference, information on the Qualtrics classic reporting is found at Appendix C of this book.

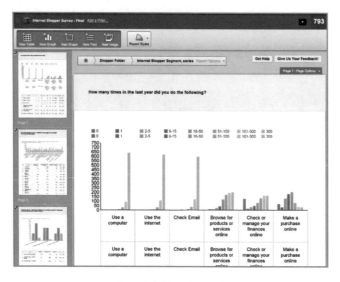

Figure 9-1 Example report.

Create a completely new report or copy an existing one.

CREATE NEW REPORTS

When you click on the Reporting Beta tab, you will be taken to the My Reports page, where you will see a list of existing reports and folders.

There are two main options for creating reports. You can create a new report or create a copy of an existing report.

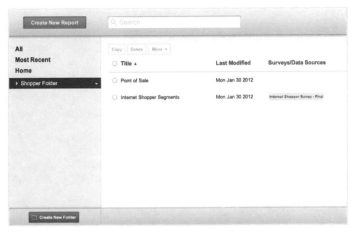

Figure 9-2 View Reports Home Page.

To create a new report:

1. Select **Create New Report**. The Create New Report dialog window will open.
2. Enter a **Report Name**. Choose a name that will make the report easy to reference later.
3. Optionally, select a **Folder** in which you would like to save the report.
4. Select the **Survey** which you would like to use for the report.

To copy an existing report:

1. Check the box next to an existing report.
2. Click the **Copy** button at the top of the list of reports.

• Organize your reports by placing them in folders. You can place the new report in an existing folder when creating it, or afterward on the reports home page. See the Folders section for more information.
• When viewing a report, you can return to the reporting home page by clicking the Home button.

FOLDERS

Just like creating folders for your surveys, you can create folders to organize and keep track of your different reports. You can even create folders within folders.

Organize your reports using folders, just like organizing surveys on the My Surveys page.

To create a new folder:

1. Click the **Create New Folder** button at the bottom left corner of the page.
2. Enter a **Folder Name** in the window that appears.
3. Click **OK**.

To create a folder within another folder, just make sure to first click the folder in the column to the left, then click the **Create New Folder** button. Your new folder will appear within the other folder.

To delete a folder:
1. In the left-hand column, click the folder you want to delete.
2. Select **Delete**.

If the folder has reports in it, you will not be able to delete it. A message will appear saying, "Cannot delete a non-empty folder. Please remove all items in the folder first." Move the reports out of that folder and try deleting it again.

To move surveys into a folder:
1. On the **My Reports** page, check the boxes next to the reports you would like to move.
2. Click the **Move** button.
3. Find and click the folder to move into.

DATA SOURCES

As the name implies, it's the source of the data used in the report. You can create filters from the Data Sources area.

A data source is simply a set of data you would like to use in your report. For example, one data source might be the results of your survey filtered to show respondents who indicate they purchase your product. Another data source might be the results of the same survey, but filtered to show those who don't purchase your product. By including both of these data sources on the same table or graph, you can compare the answers of customers to those of non-customers.

Figure 9-3 Data Sources view above report.

By default, your report will include one data source including all respondents to your survey. You can add other data sources or filter this data source as needed.

To add a new data source to your report:
1. Click the dark gray drop-down arrow on the right of an existing data source.
2. Select to Add a New Data Source.
3. Choose a survey to use for this data source.
4. The Generate Report dialog will appear.
   - Select to Create a new page for each question if you'd like new charts and graphs to be made automatically for your data source.
   - Select Merge this data source with the existing report if you'd like the new data to automatically be merged into existing charts and graphs.
   - Click Cancel if you'd like to add this data source to individual charts and graphs yourself rather than having it done automatically.

To add a data source to an individual table or graph:
1. Click on the table or graph you'd like to modify.
2. Along the top of the screen, click the Data Source drop-down menu to see which data sources are currently being used for the table of graph.
3. Click the gray plus sign to add another data source to the table or graph.
4. Choose the data source to use, and then the question to use from that data source.
   - Any two questions can be added to the same table or graph, but the information will be most useful if the two questions are similar. For instance, how much males prefer chocolate ice cream versus how much females prefer chocolate ice cream will make a more meaningful graph than how much males prefer chocolate ice cream versus how satisfied females are with their shopping experience.

TIME SERIES

Setting up a Time Series allows you to compare data across different Data Sources by date range in your Page Items.

To set up Time Series:
1. Click the drop-down menu for the Data Source.
2. Select Edit Time Series.
3. Specify how you want to set up the Time Series.
   - **LAST:** Set it up by the last number of Days, Weeks, Months, Quarters, or Years. Choose any additional options as needed:
      - **REVERSED:** Reverses the display of the intervals in the Page Items.
      - **INCLUDE THE CURRENT INTERVAL:** Whether you want to include the current day, week, month, quarter, year, or wait until the interval is over before it is included.
      - **USE CUSTOM DESCRIPTIONS:** Displays text fields for all of the intervals to be used, allowing you to enter labels for each.
   - **DATE RANGE:** Specify a date range and choose if the intervals are done by Days, Weeks, Months, Quarters, or Years. Select **Use custom descriptions** to enter custom labels for each interval.
4. Click **Save**.
5. Repeat this process for any other Data Sources you would like to use with the Time Series.

VARIABLE WEIGHTS

Adjust the weight of a particular answer choice as needed.

The Variable Weights feature allows you to assign weight to particular values of a question.

To set up variable weighting:
1. Click the drop-down menu for the Data Source.
2. Select **Variable Weights**.
3. Under **Weight Type**, specify if you want Weight, Target Percent, or Target Count.
4. Click the **Select Question** button and choose the question and answer choice.
5. In the numeric field on the left, enter the value you would like to use.
6. Use the blue plus button or click **Add a Variable Weight Logic Set** to weight additional answer choices, if desired.
7. Click **Save**.

FILTERS

Filter your report data by question response, completion status, date range, score, and embedded data.

Filters are one of the most commonly used features in reports. Often referred to as subgroups, they allow you to look at your entire data source according to how a particular question was answered or other information.

Figure 9-4 Filters view.

For example, if you ask people which color is their favorite, you can later filter the survey's data based on those who selected "blue." This allows you to get a basic idea on whether there might be a correlation between those who select "blue" and another choice selection on a different question (like members of household, level of education, etc.).

To set up a filter:
1. Click the answer choice you want to filter on.
2. Select **Create Filter From Row**.

The filter is automatically created in the Data Sources area at the top of the page. You can edit the filter as needed by changing questions and choices or by clicking the "+" or "-" buttons to add and remove lines of logic.

You can also set up a filter from the Data Sources view at the top of the page. This allows for more filtering options.

Setting up a filter in the Data Sources view:
1. In the Data Sources area, click **Add a Filter**.
2. Select how you want to filter.
   - **FILTER BY QUESTION RESPONSE:** Provide the question and answer choice for the filter.
   - **FILTER BY COMPLETION STATUS:** All responses, only Completed responses, or only Partial responses.
   - **FILTER BY DATE RANGE:** Filter the data by specific dates.
   - **SCORING:** Choose the Scoring category and show only scores equal to, greater/less than a particular value, etc.
   - **FILTER BY EMBEDDED DATA:** Specify an embedded data field name and value and show only responses equal to, not equal to, greater/less than a particular value, etc.
3. Follow the prompts entering the necessary information (question and answer choice, embedded data, date, etc.).
4. Click the gray plus button to add additional lines of logic, as needed.
5. Click **Apply the Filter**.

PAGE ITEMS

Page Items are the items you can insert into your report. These items are tables, graphs, shapes, text, and images. Unless creating a report from scratch, most desired Page Items are added when you select your Data Source and generate the report.

Insert tables, graphs, shapes, text, or images into your report.

Figure 9-5 Clicking or dragging any of these buttons allows you to insert that element.

To insert a Page Item:
1. **Click** one of the Page Items (at top left of report). Click and drag the Page Item to the page in the report if wanting more control over its placement.
   - **NEW TABLE:** To insert a table.
   - **NEW GRAPH:** To insert a graph.
   - **NEW SHAPE:** To insert a shape or background for the appearance of your page. It will basically sit behind existing elements, where you can highlight and draw attention to them by changing its color.
   - **NEW TEXT:** Use to insert text for your report viewers. Also referred to as a note.
   - **NEW IMAGE:** Drag and drop an image from your desktop directly into your report.
2. Each inserted table or graph will request you **Select Data Source** containing what you want to reference for that table or graph.
3. After you select your Data Source, select a question in the survey containing the data you want to display.

When selecting a Data Source on a table or graph, you can click the blue plus button to the right to add an additional Data Source and question. So you can have two different questions display (from two different surveys, if you choose) in the same graph.

To move a Page Item's position:
1. Click and drag the Page Item to the desired location on the report page.

- To position an element on another page, click the element and drag and drop it on the page in the page list to the left. Click the page to jump to it and adjust the element's position on that page as needed.
- If a table gets adjusted to a size smaller than the amount of data it needs to display, it will display as a torn sheet of paper at the bottom of the table to signify the need for more space.
- For more precision, use the arrow ekys on your keyboard to "nudge" the Page Item slightly in any direction.

To change the size of a Page Item:
1. **Click** on the Page Item to select it.
2. **Hover** your mouse over a corner or edge point of the Page Item.
3. **Click and drag** it to the desired size.

Press and hold **Shift** on your keyboard when you click and drag the edge point and you will keep the previous size ratio of the Page Item when dragging.

To copy an existing Page Item:
1. Press and hold **Alt** on your keyboard (**Option** key if using a Mac).
2. **Click and drag** the Page Item. A duplicate Page Item will break away from the original, which you can then move and edit as needed.

To delete a Page Item:
1. Click to select the Page Item.
2. Click the **Remove Page** Item button at the top right of the report.

If you have selected the element, you can also use the **Delete** or **Backspace** keys on your keyboard, or even right click the Page Item and select **Remove Item**.

To group multiple Page Items:

1. Press and hold the **Shift** key on your keyboard.
2. **Click** to select the different Page Items you want to group. Now that the items are grouped, you can move and resize them together.

- You can also click and drag your mouse to highlight all the different Page Items (rather than Shift+clicking).
- You can only group items that appear on the same page.
- Holding Shift while dragging to resize the group will keep the previous size ratio of the grouped items.

PAGE ITEM OPTIONS

Though there is no specific Page Item Options menu, when you click a Page Item, various menus specific to that item are available at the top of the report. You can also right click the Page Item to see many of the same options.

These are editing options specific to the selected Page Item.

Something to note is when a Page Item is selected, the menu options at the top of the report will only apply to the selected Page Item. If no Page Item is selected, you can click Report Styles and use Graph Options and Table Options to adjust all graphs or tables across the entire report. The Report Styles menu also allows you to adjust the font, font size, and font color across all Page Items in the report.

TABLES

When you click a table, the following buttons are available for customizing the table and choosing the desired type of table.

Figure 9-6 Table specific buttons available when a table is selected.

- **DATA SOURCE:** This allows you to add or remove questions, or Data Sources, for that particular table. You can also access this by right clicking the table.
- **TABLE TYPE:** There are five potential types to choose from.
    - **DEFAULT:** The default selection, which shows the choices, the number of responses, and the percent of responses for each choice.
    - **STATISTICS:** This table shows basic statistics, which show Min Value, Max Value, Mean, Variance, Standard Deviation, and number of Respondents.
    - **TABLE OTHER TEXT:** This shows the entered text if there is a text entry choice, like an "Other" option.
    - **TEXT ANALYSIS:** Displays a table of the top ten words used and the count of their usage. Clicking View More will display a comprehensive list, which can be exported to Excel (.xls).

- **CROSS TAB:** If you have created a Cross Tab in the Cross Tabulation area of the tool, you can select it here and display it in your report.
- **TABLE OPTIONS:** Use this table to change the look and feel of the table, including font and decimal places. These options are also available by right clicking the table.
  - **FONT:** Change the font style, size, and color.
  - **LOOK AND FEEL:** Choose a thumbnail at the top of the menu to change the general appearance of the graph.
  - **DECIMAL PLACES:** Choose how many decimal places are used when displaying values, from zero to five or No Limit on the decimals. Two is the default selection.
  - **TRANSPOSE:** Reverse the columns and rows of the table. This can be quite useful if you transposed a matrix table on the Edit Survey page.
  - **SORT BY:** Choose a column (typically an answer choice) by which to sort the table.
  - **SHOW/HIDE COLUMNS:** Choose to display or not display certain columns in the table.
  - **SHOW/HIDE ROWS:** Choose to display or not display certain rows in the table.
  - **DATA FORMAT:** Base the table off the Count, Percent, or Mean.
  - **UNIFORM CELLS:** Adjusts the size of each cell to be equal in size. By default, the columns are unequal in width.
  - **EXPAND TO HEIGHT:** Selected by default, this option spaces out the table to take up the amount of space the table is allotted.
  - **EXPORT TABLE TO:** Export the table to PDF, Microsoft Excel, Microsoft Powerpoint, or Microsoft Word.
  - **CLEAR PROPERTIES:** Remove all applied settings in Table Options and use default settings.
- **LAYOUT:** Basic formatting options for the table.
  - **SHOW ON ALL PAGES:** Show the selected table on all pages of the report.
  - **ALWAYS ON TOP:** Specify if you want the table to display on top of any other Page Item it might conflict with on other pages.
  - **ALWAYS ON BOTTOM:** Specify if you want the table to display beneath any other Page Item it might conflict with on other pages.
  - **ADD DESCRIPTION:** Automatically adds the question text for the question it represents. Double click the text to edit as needed.
  - **CENTER WITHIN PAGE HORIZONTAL:** Automatically centers the table horizontally on the page.
  - **CENTER WITHIN PAGE VERTICAL:** Automatically centers the table vertically on the page.
  - **REAPPLY LAYOUT:** After making changes, you can apply the original layout back to the table using this option.

Tables also provide the ability to adjust the column headers. Click on a table heading and you can choose between Header Options and Column Options.

- **HEADER OPTIONS:** Adjust font style, font size, font color, and even rename the header.
- **COLUMN OPTIONS:** Adjust cell text alignment to left, center, or right. The Bar area of the table will let you change the bar color.

- If a table gets adjusted to a size smaller than the amount of data it needs to display, it will display as a torn sheet of paper at the bottom of the table to signify the need for more space.
- Right click the graph for most of the same items, as well as some additional items, like creating a drill down report from that item.

GRAPHS

When you click to select a graph, the following buttons are available for choosing the desired type of graph and additional customization.

Figure 9-7 Graph specific buttons available when a graph is selected.

- **DATA SOURCE:** This allows you to add or remove questions, or data sources, from the graph. Clicking the graph icon on the far left brings up the Graph Options menu, specific to that Data Source.
- **GRAPH TYPE:** Choose from over thirty different graph options.
- **GRAPH OPTIONS:** Use this to change various options for the graph.
  - **FONT:** Change the font style, size, and color.
  - **COLORS:** Change the graph's colors.
  - **3D DEPTH:** Adjust the thickness of the 3D aspect of the graph's columns or elements.
  - **OPACITY:** The amount of transparency or translucence with which to display the graph.
  - **SHOW VALUES:** Have the choice values display on the graph elements.
  - **TRUNCATE LABELS:** This will cut short the longer choice labels to make more room for the rest of the graph view.
  - **REVERSE DATA LAYERS:** This looks at your data sources you are using in your graph and reverses their order from top to bottom. This change adjusts the display of the graph because the order of the data layers controls which data sources display first, second, etc.
  - **SWAP LABELS WITH LEGEND KEYS:** Uses a Legend to label the graph instead of labeling along the graph axis.
  - **USE MULTI-COLORED BARS:** Rather than using one color for all graph bars, the graph displays unique colors for each bar. Swap Labels With Legend Keys automatically does this.
  - **AXIS AND GRID LINES:** By default, the X and Y axes display. You can choose to turn off the X and Y axes, display X and Y grid lines, as well as hide the Label and Number axes.
  - **AXIS SCALE LIMIT:** Set a custom scale limit instead of letting the graph automatically choose the axis scale. This typically refers to the Y axis.
  - **DECIMAL PLACES:** Choose how many decimal places are used when displaying

values, from zero to five or No Limit on the decimals. Two is the default selection.

- **SORT DATA BY:** Choose to sort the graph by Choices, Series, Labels, and Keys.
- **SHOW/HIDE COLUMNS:** Choose to display or not display certain columns in the graph.
- **DATA FORMAT:** Choose if the graph should be based off the response Count, Percent, Mean, or Standard Deviation.
- **CLEAR PROPERTIES:** Remove all applied settings in Graph Options and use default settings.

- **LAYOUT:** Basic formatting options for the graph.
  - **SHOW ON ALL PAGES:** Show the selected graph on all pages of the report.
  - **ALWAYS ON TOP:** Specify if you want the graph to display on top of any other Page Item it might conflict with on other pages.
  - **ALWAYS ON BOTTOM:** Specify if you want the graph to display beneath any other Page Item it might conflict with on other pages.
  - **ADD DESCRIPTION:** Automatically adds the question text for the question it represents. Double click the text to edit as needed.
  - **CENTER WITHIN PAGE HORIZONTAL:** Automatically centers the graph horizontally on the page.
  - **CENTER WITHIN PAGE VERTICAL:** Automatically centers the graph vertically on the page.
  - **REAPPLY LAYOUT:** After making changes, you can apply the original layout back to the graph using this option.

Q-TIP

- Right click the graph for most of the same items, as well as some additional items, like exporting the graph or creating a drill down report from that question.
- Change a graph's labels by clicking directly on them.

SHAPE

Shapes can be used to highlight particular Page Items in your report.

Figure 9-8 Shape specific buttons available when a shape is selected.

- **SHAPE STYLES:** Use Shape Styles to give the shape rounded corners or change the Background Color or Border Color. Click the color square to open a color palette where you can choose a specific color for the background or border.
- **LAYOUT:** Basic formatting options for the shape.
  - **SHOW ON ALL PAGES:** Show the selected shape on all pages of the report.
  - **ALWAYS ON TOP:** Specify if you want the shape to display on top of any other Page Item it might conflict with on other pages.
  - **ALWAYS ON BOTTOM:** Specify if you want the shape to display beneath any other Page Item it might conflict with on other pages.

- **CENTER WITHIN PAGE HORIZONTAL:** Automatically centers the shape horizontally on the page.
- **CENTER WITHIN PAGE VERTICAL:** Automatically centers the shape vertically on the page.
- **REAPPLY LAYOUT:** After making changes, you can apply the original layout back to the shape using this option.

TEXT

Inserting a Text item allows you to insert a note into your report. These Text items are how the report automatically inserts question text and page numbers. When a Text item is selected, there are various options available.

Figure 9-9 Text specific buttons available when a text Page Item is selected.

- **DATA SOURCE:** Choose the type of Text item you would like to display.
    - **TEXT:** This is useful for entering your own notes and text.
    - **SURVEY QUESTION:** Choose this option to display question text.
    - **PAGE INFORMATION:** Display a Page Number, Export Tag, or Page Description. This option is also available by right clicking the Text item.
    - **ITEM INFORMATION:** Pull in the appropriate text information for the selected item (Text, Graph, Table, Shape). For example, Graph and Table will pull in the appropriate question text.
- **TEXT OPTIONS:** Various options can be adjusted using the Text Options menu.
    - **FONT:** Choose a font style, font size, and font color for the text of the Text item.
    - **BOLD:** Add or remove bold formatting to the entire text. This is applied by default.
    - **ITALICS:** Add or remove italic formatting to the entire text.
    - **BACKGROUND COLOR:** Change default gray shading behind the question text to a different color. This is similar to having a shape always behind the text.
    - **BORDER COLOR:** Change default gray border to a different color.
    - **ROUNDED CORNERS:** Round the corners of the background field behind the text.
    - **PADDING:** Adjust the spacing around the text within the background color or shape.
    - **ALIGNMENT:** Left, Center, or Right align the text in the Text item.
    - **VERTICAL ALIGNMENT:** Top, Middle, or Bottom align the text in the Text item.
    - **CLEAR PROPERTIES:** Remove all applied settings in Text Options and use default settings.
- **LAYOUT:** Basic formatting options for the text.
    - **SHOW ON ALL PAGES:** Show the selected text on all pages of the report.
    - **ALWAYS ON TOP:** Specify if you want the text to display on top of any other Page Item it might conflict with on other pages.
    - **ALWAYS ON BOTTOM:** Specify if you want the text to display beneath any other Page Item it might conflict with on other pages.

- **CENTER WITHIN PAGE HORIZONTAL:** Automatically centers the text horizontally on the page.
- **CENTER WITHIN PAGE VERTICAL:** Automatically centers the text vertically on the page.
- **REAPPLY LAYOUT:** After making changes, you can apply the original layout back to the text using this option.

Click **Edit Text** just above the text item or double click the text to open the Rich Content Editor and edit the text.

PAGE OPTIONS

At the top right corner of each page of the report is a gray button (Page # - Page Options). You can click this button to see page options. You can also find these options by right clicking the page's thumbnail image in the table of contents to the left.

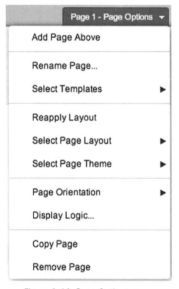

Figure 9-10 Page Options menu.

- **ADD PAGE ABOVE:** Insert a blank page above the existing page.
- **RENAME PAGE:** Allows you to rename the page, using something more descriptive than just "Page 2," etc.
- **SELECT TEMPLATES:**
  - **NONE:** No template is applied.
  - **USE ALL TEMPLATES:** Selected by default, this applies all templates to the page.
  - **MAKE ALL PAGES LIKE THIS:** Creates a template and applies it to all other pages in the report.

- **MANAGE TEMPLATES:** Opens the Template Manager window to create new templates and edit existing templates. In the Template Manager you can adjust the margins, and border color and thickness.
- **REAPPLY LAYOUT:** Reapplies the layout after changes have been made.
- **SELECT PAGE LAYOUT:** Select a specific page layout. These are the same layouts available when you generate your report.
- **SELECT PAGE THEME:** Choose no theme or use the default Qualtrics theme, which is the basic formatting around the question text.
- **PAGE ORIENTATION:** Toggle between Portrait (default) and Landscape paper orientation.
- **DISPLAY LOGIC:** This opens a Display Logic window like you see on the Edit Survey page. You can control a page's display in the Web View depending on the statistics for a particular question. This is useful with a page containing a text item explaining the situation, whether positive or negative.
- **COPY PAGE:** Make an exact copy of the page, which you can edit as needed.
- **REMOVE PAGE:** Deletes the page and its included Page Items.

REPORT OPTIONS

Report Options are found by clicking the report's name at the top of the report next to the Home button. This is where you can find various options, like the page size, as well as exporting, renaming, and copying the report.

Options for the entire report, like page size, orientation, and numbering, as well as setting up a Web View, scheduling a report email, or exporting the report.

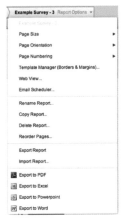

Figure 9-11 Report Options menu found by clicking report name.

- **PAGE SIZE:** Letter is the default page size, but you can choose from **ISO A Series**, **North American**, and custom **Powerpoint** sizes.
- **PAGE ORIENTATION:** Choose between Portrait (default) and Landscape page orientation for the entire report.
- **PAGE NUMBERING:** Choose to number your report pages sequentially or by Export Tags. No page numbering is the default selection.

- **TEMPLATE MANAGER (BORDERS & MARGINS):** This opens a window allowing you to assign a margin and border around the report.
- **WEB VIEW:** Also known as a Public Report, this turns your report into a web page. Click Enable to get the link. The Web View will display your Page Items with the latest data each time the page is loaded, including filtered data.
    - **PASSWORD PROTECTION:** Select this option to assign a password to your Web View, so only those with the password can view the report.
- **EMAIL SCHEDULER:** Use this option to schedule a weekly or monthly email with one of the report export options attached.
- **RENAME REPORT:** Edit the report's name.
- **COPY REPORT:** Copy an existing report and all of its Page Items, etc.
- **DELETE REPORT:** Delete an existing report. You will be asked to confirm deletion. You can also delete report from the reports Home page by checking the box next to the report(s) and clicking the Delete button.
- **REORDER PAGES:** This opens a new view of thumbnail graphics of each report page. Click and drag each page into the order you desire.
- **EXPORT REPORT:** Exports the report as a file in the Qualtrics Report Format (.qrf), which you can save or email as needed.
- **IMPORT REPORT:** Allows you to select a downloaded report file (.qrf) to import as a new report.
- **EXPORT:** Export your entire report to PDF, Excel, Powerpoint, or Word format.

Responses

The Responses page of the View Results tab has various purposes. It is useful for deleting test data, viewing individual response information, viewing basic information of responses in progress, as well as importing data.

Figure 9-12 Responses button under View Results tab.

There are two tabs in the Responses page where you can find information. These tabs are Recorded Responses and Responses in Progress.

Figure 9-13 Recorded Responses page.

RECORDED RESPONSES

Recorded Responses is commonly used for viewing individual responses, deleting test data, and importing data. At the top of the Recorded Responses page are the search criteria options that can be used to search through the individual responses. You can search by the following criteria. The more criteria you enter, the more specific your search will be.

Verify your data by viewing the Recorded Responses page.

- **RESPONSE TYPE:**
    - **IP ADDRESS:** The IP Address is grabbed for the legitimate survey responses, which are those coming from one of the options on the Distribute Survey tab.
    - **PANEL:** This filters for those who took the survey from an email invitation on the Email Survey page.
    - **IMPORTED:** These are responses that were imported into the tool. Responses are imported using Advanced Options.
    - **SURVEY TEST:** These are test responses using the Test Survey tool found on the Edit Survey page under Advanced Options.
    - **SURVEY PREVIEW:** These are test responses from using the Preview Survey button, which is found on the My Survey, Edit Survey, and Distribute Survey tabs.
    - **SPAM:** The tool looks at responses that come from the same IP Address within the last 24 hours and marks them as spam. This isn't a guarantee that they are spam, but more of a notification the response(s) could be spam. This is also designated by an "8" in the Status column when you download your data on the Download Data page.
    - **NOT SPAM:** This will filter for those not marked as spam according to the criteria explained above.
- **FROM DATE:** This refers to the Start Date column in the table below on the page, as well as from the data downloads.
- **END DATE:** This refers to the End Date column in the table below on the page, as well as from the data downloads.
- **FIRST NAME:** First name of individual.
- **LAST NAME:** Last name of individual.
- **EMAIL ADDRESS:** Email address of individual.

- **EXTERNAL REFERENCE:** This is the External Data Reference you may have used when importing a panel.
- **RESPONSE ID:** Search for a specific Response ID among your data set.

RESPONSE TABLE

Below the search fields is a table of all responses stored in the system. It is here that you can view individual responses and delete data.

There are six columns in the table providing information and useful tools:

- **RESPONSE ID:** This is the ID used in the Qualtrics database to keep track of each individual response in the system. Click the Response ID to open a window to view the individual's response. From this view you have the ability to export the individual's response to PDF.
- **RESPONDENT:** This will show the respondent's name (if part of a panel) or IP Address. If the response is a different type of response, it will show the Response Type.
- **RESPONSE TYPE:** This is the type of response, telling you whether it is an actual response, test response, or imported response.
  - **IP ADDRESS:** This displays for those taking the survey from the anonymous survey link or a panel link.
  - **IMPORTED RESPONSE:** Displays just for those responses that were imported using the Advanced Options menu. For more information on importing responses, see the Import Responses section coming up.
  - **SURVEY PREVIEW:** These are responses that came in from the Preview Survey and View buttons found on the My Surveys, Edit Survey, and Distribute Survey tabs.
  - **SURVEY TEST:** Responses that came in using the Test Survey tool found in the Edit Survey and View Results pages.
- **START TIME:** When the survey was started according to your time zone selected under Account Settings.
- **END TIME:** When the survey finished or the last time the respondent accessed the survey if it was closed due to the partial data setting. This is according to your time zone selected under Account Settings.
- **DURATION:** Subtracting the Start Time from the End Time.
- **ACTIONS:** The Actions menu provides two options for retaking the survey.
  - **RETAKE SURVEY:** This provides a new survey link. Clicking the link starts at the beginning of the survey with all questions showing their selection, which can be changed (this is the way editing is completed). For this response to be accepted, click completely through the survey. Once completed, the new answers will replace the previous responses.
  - **RETAKE SURVEY AS NEW RESPONSE:** This provides a new survey link. Clicking the link starts at the beginning of the survey with all questions showing their selection. Respond to all questions and complete the survey. The new responses will not replace the old response, but instead a new response will be added in addition to the old response.

There are four buttons across the top of the respondent data table.

- **ALL:** Select all responses on the page.
- **NONE:** Remove selection of all responses on the page.
- **VIEW:** Clicking View will open a window and display all selected responses. If you select multiple responses, it will display their individual responses side by side. The selected responses can be exported to PDF, which will export as one long file containing all of the selected responses.
- **ALL + DELETE:** Allows you to delete all selected responses. You will be prompted to confirm the deletion.

To delete individual responses:

1. On the Recorded Responses page, click the **checkboxes** of the responses you want to delete.
2. Click the **Delete** button at the top of the table of responses.

- Use the **All** button at the top of the response table if you want to select and delete all responses on that page.
- Use the **Advanced Options** drop-down menu to delete all responses or specific types of responses. See the Delete Data Options section later in this chapter.

ADVANCED OPTIONS

The Advanced Options menu provides some additional options for importing and deleting responses on the Recorded Responses page.

IMPORT RESPONSES

You can import data from the same survey, from another survey, and even from a survey that originated in another survey tool or data collection method.

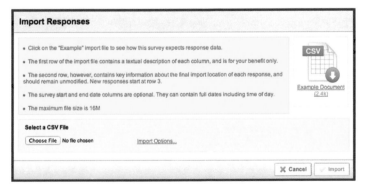

Figure 9-154 Import Responses dialog window.

To import responses:
1. On the Recorded Responses page, click **Advanced Options** and select **Import Responses**.
2. Click **Choose File** (or Browse) and select the file containing the response data. The imported file must be a .csv (Comma Separated Values) format, which you can Save As in Excel and most spreadsheet applications.
3. Make sure the columns and their headers correctly match in the preview.
4. When ready, click the **Import** button.

Q-TIP

- Use the **Import Options** button if the imported file's preview is not displaying correctly. You can specify the correct **Delimiter** (select or type in) and **Enclosure** (select or type in). **Do not validate** will ignore Required Response on any questions in the survey, in case there are responses that were skipped due to logic (skip, display, branch).
- Click the **Example Document** button at the top right of the Import Responses dialog to download a custom example file specific to your survey.
- If importing a data file from **another survey tool**, you will need to match up the columns with what the Qualtrics Survey Research Suite is expecting. The Example Document download is an extremely useful tool in seeing the Question IDs and other column headers the tool expects.

GENERATE TEST RESPONSES

Generate Test Responses allows you to test your survey by adding dummy data to your questions. This Test Survey option is also found under the Advanced Options drop-down menu on the Edit Survey tab. For more information, see the Test Survey explanation under Advanced Options in the Edit Survey chapter.

DELETE DATA OPTIONS

While you can delete your data by selecting the checkboxes and clicking the Delete button, there are four specialized options for deleting certain types of data.

- **DELETE SURVEY PREVIEWS:** Deletes only "Preview" responses that came from previewing the Survey (through the Survey Preview link).
- **DELETE SURVEY TESTS:** Deletes only test responses that came from the Test Survey tool.
- **DELETE IMPORTED RESPONSES:** Delete only responses imported on the Recorded Responses page.
- **DELETE ALL RESPONSES:** Delete all of the survey's data up to that point in time, regardless of the type of data.

Surveys being taken or otherwise incomplete are displayed here. Includes the last question answered and general survey progress.

RESPONSES IN PROGRESS

The Responses in Progress page shows respondent surveys that are open (started, but unfinished, surveys). These are active responses not yet completed or not yet closed by the partial data time frame.

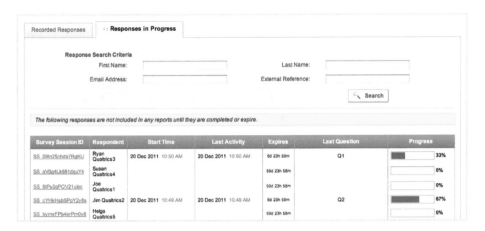

Figure 9-15 Responses in Progress page.

There are four search fields you can use to search for Responses in Progress: first name, last name, email address, and external reference number. These four fields are also found under Recorded Responses and are explained there.

The Responses in Progress table contains seven columns of information:
- **SURVEY SESSION ID:** This is the ID the Qualtrics database uses to keep track of this individual response. Click this ID to display the individual's question responses entered so far. This can be exported to PDF as well.
- **RESPONDENT:** This is respondent-specific information, like name (if available from a panel) or IP Address.
- **START TIME:** The time the respondent started the survey.
- **LAST ACTIVITY:** The last time the respondent accessed the survey. This time will update to the most recent time the survey was accessed.
- **EXPIRES:** When the survey session will expire. At first this pertains to when the email will expire (set under Advanced Options on Email Survey page). Once the link is clicked it pertains to the partial data time frame under Survey Options and how much time is remaining from the Last Activity date/time.
- **LAST QUESTION:** The most recent question answered by the respondent.
- **PROGRESS:** A percent of the respondent's progress through the survey so far.

The table has respondent selection options available in the list of buttons at the top of the table:
- **ALL:** Select all responses on the page: for use in Close Responses or Delete buttons.
- **NONE:** Removes all selection of responses on that page.
- **CLOSE RESPONSES:** Closes the survey session and stores the response as partial data. This is the same as manually activating the partial data time frame under Survey Options. If there is no data for any question in the response at the time, then it will not store it as partial data.
    - Under Survey Options, if **Do not record partially completed surveys** is selected, the closed response will not be stored.
- **DELETE:** Completely deletes the response in progress. This deletion means the survey session is also closed.

◻ Download Data

*Need an SPSS,
Excel, CSV,
XML or HTML
file for another
application?
Export the
survey data
directly into
a native file
for these
applications.*

The Download Data page is where to go when needing to export your data to an external application. There are various download options available (Figure 9-16).

- **CSV:** A comma separated values file that can be opened in Excel and many other applications.
- **SPSS:** A .sav file specifically for SPSS.
    - If having trouble using the SPSS export file, select a different string width option in the menu depending on your version of SPSS.
    - If you prefer a syntax file, click the **Download SPSS Syntax File** button on the far right.
- **FIXED-FIELD-LENGTH FORMAT:** A .zip file containing a text (.txt) file of data and a .csv file containing the data map. This options is designed specifically for market research firms.
- **XML:** XML stands for eXtensible Markup Language and is commonly used for putting data into databases and similar tools, especially when automating the download process.
- **HTML:** Displays the data in an HTML table in a separate browser window/tab.

Figure 9-16 Download Data page.

Q-TIP

- If you are not able to download all of the data you expect, check to see if a subgroup is applied or if an incorrect response set is selected. You can see this information near the top right corner of the page. Any changes made to these two items are done while viewing your report.
- Remember downloading your data does not remove the data from the Qualtrics database. It is still accessible in your account for viewing in the reports and for downloading again later, if you choose.
- **Excel 2003** and earlier has a limit of 256 columns and 65,536 rows. **Excel 2007** and later supports 16,384 columns and 1,048,676 rows. If your data exceeds the capacity of your version of Excel, you will need to download the data in multiple sets, which is usually best done

downloading only certain questions and/or by limiting your information downloaded using a subgroup filter in the reports.
- Different versions of **SPSS** also have similar limits you will need to be careful about. Check your SPSS version's documentation for more information on any limitations you might find.

Cross Tabulation

A Cross Tabulation is a table used for comparing the data of various questions or embedded data to determine if there is a relationship between the variables being compared (Figure 9-17). Many options are available that allow you to select which types of summary data appear in the tables.

Bivariate or multivariate cross tabs are used to explore percentage and statistical relationships between multiple questions.

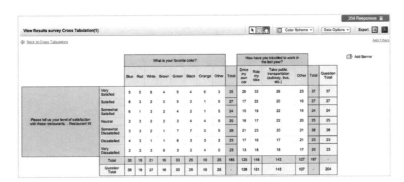

Figure 9-17 A Basic Cross Tabulation Table.

To create a new Cross Tabulation:
1. On the Cross Tabulation page, click the **Create a New Cross Tabulation** button.
2. Give your Cross Tabulation a name for later reference.
3. In the menu that displays, choose the questions or embedded data to be your **Banners** (Columns) and **Stubs** (Rows).
- Banners: This is the information going across the top as the columns.
- Stubs: This is the information going down the side as the rows.
4. If you have Embedded Data in your survey, you may click **Use Embedded Data** near the bottom of the list of questions to choose any fields for the Cross Tabulation.
    1. Choose whether the embedded data field is to be used as a banner or stub.
    2. Click the **AutoFill** button to pull in the values.
    3. Remove any values you don't want to use.
5. When ready, click **Create Cross Tabulation**.

To add additional Banners or Stubs to existing Cross Tabulation (multiple variables may appear in each table, as shown in Figure 9-17):

1. Click to view an existing Cross Tabulation.
2. Click **Add Banner** or **Add Stub**.
   - Add Banner (to right of Cross Tab) adds an additional Banner or column variable.
   - Add Stub (at bottom of Cross Tab) adds an additional Stub or row variable.
3. Click the question or embedded data field to add.
   - If embedded data field is selected, remember to click AutoFill and then remove any undesired values.
4. Click **Recalculate Cross Tabulation**.

CROSS TAB TABLE OPTIONS

To find the Table Options, in an existing Cross Tabulation, hover your mouse over the question text and click the down arrow.

Figure 9-18 Cross Tab Table Options menu.

- **ADD MULTILEVEL DRILL DOWN:** Nests a question within each level of the main banner or stub as an additional level of comparison.
   1. Select **Add Multilevel Drill Down**.
   2. Click the question to add.
   3. Click **Recalculate Cross Tabulation**.
- **DELETE BANNER/STUB:** Removes the selected banner or stub variable.
   1. Select Delete Banner or Delete Stub.
   2. Click **Recalculate Cross Tabulation**.
- **MERGE:** Combines two or more answer choices into a single value in the Cross Tab. The values will be summed.
   1. Select **Merge**.
   2. Click the choices to combine.
   3. Click **Merge** button. Click **Unmerge** to undo a Merge.
   4. Click **Save**.
   5. Click **Recalculate Cross Tabulation**.

Though not specifically an option, edit the label by clicking the question text or an answer choice. This is useful for shortening question text and answer choices having long text descriptions.

CROSS TABULATION FILTERS

Apply a subgroup filter to your Cross Tabulation like you can in your reports.

Figure 9-19 Simple filter set up on a Cross Tabulation.

To apply a filter:
1. Click **Add Filters** button (located above Cross Tabulation table on the far right side).
2. Choose in the first menu if it should be based on a Question or Embedded Data.
   - If **Question**:
      1. Select the question.
      2. Select the answer choice.
      3. Specify the condition (whether the choice is selected or not selected).

   - If **Embedded Data**:
      1. Enter the Embedded Data field name.
      2. Specify the condition (Greater/Less Than, etc.).
      3. Enter the field's value.
3. Click the blue "+" button to add additional logic to your Filter.
4. Click **Recalculate Cross Tabulation**.

CROSS TABULATION OPTIONS

At the top of the Cross Tabulations screen are the various options for selecting cells in the Cross Tab, Color Schemes, Data Options, and export options.

Figure 9-20 Cross Tabulation Options.

- **ROW/COLUMN SELECTOR (ARROW):** Clicking any cell highlights the cell's associated column and row.
- **CUSTOM HIGHLIGHTER (YELLOW BOX):** Clicking any cell highlights the cell in bright yellow to make sure it stands out.
   - Use Data Highlighter under Data Options to set up additional highlighting options where you don't have to manually click particular cells. See Data Highlighter below for more information.
- **GRABBER TOOL:** Use the hand cursor to click and drag the Cross Tabulation to the position you desire.
- **COLOR SCHEME:** There are 11 different color scheme options to choose from. The default selection is Olive.

- **DATA OPTIONS:**
  - **FREQUENCIES:** Selected by default. This is the number of times the column/row matchup has occurred for the corresponding answer choices.
  - **EXPECTED FREQUENCIES:** A presumed frequency expected to occur.
  - **ACTUAL–EXPECTED:** The Expected Frequency subtracted from the actual Frequency.
  - **ROW PERCENT:** Cell's Frequency compared to the Row's Total (Frequency / Row Total).
  - **COLUMN PERCENT:** Cell's Frequency compared to the Column's Total (Frequency / Column Total).
  - **SHOW BANNER MEANS:** The column's Mean. This is calculated by summing each Frequency in the column (times its answer choice value from the Stub or row) and dividing the sum by the Banner's Total. *Example: [(Freq 1 x 1)+(Freq 2 x 2)+(Freq 3 + 3)] / Banner Total.*
  - **SHOW STUB MEANS:** The row's Mean. This is calculated by summing each Frequency in the row (times its answer choice value from the Banner or column), divided by the Stub's Total. *Example: [(Freq 1 x 1)+(Freq 2 x 2)+(Freq 3 + 3)] / Stub Total.*
  - **SHOW QUESTION TOTALS:** This is the sheer total of times the answer choice was selected (referring to its corresponding column or row Question Total).
  - **SHOW TOTALS:** Selected by default, this displays a total after each question. It is the sum of the Frequency of combination of the two compared questions.
  - **SHOW RECODED VALUES:** This shows the answer choice values being used for each answer choice. The value appears in parentheses below the choice label.
  - **DECIMALS:** The number of decimals displayed for each count. Two is the default selection. This affects Expected Frequencies, Actual – Expected, Row Percents, Column Percents, Banner Means, and Stub Means.
  - **DATA HIGHLIGHTER:** Choose a Data Option, Data Highlighter, and then a condition, a value to compare, and a color. Click the "+" button to the right to add additional highlighting options.
    - Within the Data Highlighter menu, Preset Highlighter options can be accessed from the Select a Preset dropdown menu. A legend explaining the colors will display below the Cross Tab.
    - Remove the applied highlighting by clicking the **Clear Highlights** button directly above the Cross Tabulation.
  - **ADVANCED OPTIONS:** Presents the options for calculating the number of responses (respondents or responses) and whether to display or not display non-responses.
    - **CALCULATE STATS BASED ON RESPONDENTS:** The stats and percentages are based on the number of respondents. This is the default selection.
    - **CALCULATE STATS BASED ON RESPONSES:** The percentages and stats are based on the number of responses. This method is typically not recommended because multiple answer questions can have more responses to the question than the total respondents answering the question.
    - **IGNORE NON-RESPONSES:** This ignores responses where the respondent didn't answer the particular question. This is the default selection.
    - **SHOW NON-RESPONSES:** An additional column is shown for each question showing the number of respondents who did not answer the question.
- **EXPORT:** Click the associated icon to export the Cross Tabulation to Excel (.xls) or PDF.

CROSS TABULATION STATISTICS

Below the Cross Tabulation is a comparison showing Chi-Square, Degrees of Freedom, and p-value.

		What is your favorite color?	How have you travelled to work in the last year?
Please tell us your level of satisfaction with these restaurants. - Restaurant W	Chi Square	52.19*	10.64
	Degrees of Freedom	42	18
	p-value	0.13	0.91

*Note: The Chi-Square approximation may be inaccurate - expected frequency less than 5.

Figure 9-21 Cross Tabulation Statistics example.

- **CHI-SQUARE:** A statistic based on the differences between the expected and observed frequencies of a variable. It is used to determine if there is a relationship between two variables.
  - **ALERT:** The Chi-Square approximation may be inaccurate when the expected frequency of a given cell is less than 5.
- **DEGREES OF FREEDOM:** The difference between the sample size and the number of parameters you're estimating. The full implications of the number of degrees of freedom are very complex. Generally, however, larger degrees of freedom allow for more precision in parameter estimates. (This is why sample size is so important.)
- **P-VALUE:** The chance an observed relationship is pure chance. A 0.01 p-value means there is a 1% chance that a relationship observed to be statistically significant is, in fact, not significant. In statistical terms, this is the probability of making a type I error, or the mistake of finding a relationship when none exists.

Summary

After collecting your data through the research suite, your next priority is to accurately assess what the data is telling you. In this chapter, we went over the options you have in the tool for analyzing your data. You can create a custom report in your account with tables and graphs or export the data to Excel or SPSS for more advanced analysis.

If you choose to create a report in your account, you can filter the reports to only include portions of your data. For example, you can create a report with only data from female respondents and create a report from only male respondents. Once you are done customizing, you can easily export your report, or use the public report link option to share your report online.

For more advanced analysis, you can use the Cross Tabulation feature to compare different variables of your data to see if there is any correlation between them. It's much like creating a pivot table in Excel. Cross tabulations can also be exported as various file types so you can easily include them in any of your own reports or presentations.

Question Types

Qualtrics gives you many different ways to ask a question. This is a quick overview of your options and will help you find the best questions for your study.

Changing the Question Type

More than 100 question types give you the flexibility to collect the information you need.

Change the question type of a question by selecting the question (it turns blue), then clicking the green **Change Item Type** button to the right of the question in the blue question menu bar. When a question type is selected, the options in the blue question menubar to the right adjust according to that question type. A detailed description of each Question Type is given in the next section of this chapter.

ALERT: If you've already begun collecting responses, changing your question type could result in the loss of collected data.

Q-TIP

- The Show All Question Types option appears at the bottom of the Question Types menu, and displays the available variations of each question type. It includes additional question types that are not visible in the main question type menu.
- Once you've selected a question type, the Question Type menu closes. You can now edit your question and return to editing other questions in the survey.
- Even after your questions have been edited, you can change the question type.

ALERT: If you've already begun collecting responses, changing your question type could result in the loss of collected data. Please be careful changing question type after you have started to collect your data. If you delete an answer choice, all data attached to that answer choice will be deleted.

Multiple Choice

Standard multiple choice question type.

This is the most frequently used question type. The Multiple Choice question allows the respondent to choose one or multiple options from the list of choices, as shown in Figure A-1.

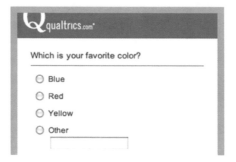

Figure A-1 The most common question type, a single answer multiple choice question.

VARIATIONS OF THE MULTIPLE CHOICE QUESTION:

Answers

- **SINGLE ANSWER:** Uses radio buttons. The standard single-select option.
- **MULTIPLE ANSWER:** Uses checkboxes. Respondents can select more than one choice.
- **DROP-DOWN LIST:** Places choices in a drop-down list. This option is *only* a single answer option.
- **SELECT BOX:** Places answer choices in an item selection box. A single option can be selected.
- **MULTI SELECT BOX:** Places choices in an item selection box. Multiple answers can be selected.

Position
Only visible when Single Answer or Multiple Answer is selected.

- **VERTICAL:** Aligns choices vertically.
- **HORIZONTAL:** Aligns choices horizontally.
- **COLUMN:** Aligns choices in columns and allows you to specify the number of columns in which answers are to be displayed.

Matrix Table

Matrix table questions are also very popular. This question type allows you to ask many multiple choice questions that use the same answer choice scale. This is a great way to save space and shorten the appearance of your survey (Figure 4-2).

How would you rate the food quality of the following restaurants?

	Excellent	Good	Average	Fair	Poor
McDonald's	○	○	○	○	○
Wendy's	○	○	○	○	○
In-N-Out	○	○	○	○	○

Figure A-2 Example of the Matrix Table Likert question type.

Likert, Semantic Differential, Rank Order and Constant Sum question options are but a few formatting options. Matrix tables combine multiple choice questions using the same scale or choices.

VARIATIONS OF THE MATRIX TABLE QUESTION:

Matrix Type

- **LIKERT:** Allows you to label the scale of choices across the top.
- **BIPOLAR:** Also known as a Semantic Differential, allows you to place two opposite choices on either side of a scale. The respondent can then choose from the options in between the two bipolar scale points.
- **RANK ORDER:** Combines the Matrix and the Rank Order question types. It allows respondents to type in a ranking for each scale point as it applies to each statement.
- **CONSTANT SUM:** Combines the Matrix and Constant Sum question types. It allows respondents to type in a value for each scale points. The sum is totaled at the end of each row.
- **TEXT ENTRY:** Combines the Matrix and Text Entry question types. It allows respondents to type in comments and other information for each specific scale point. The length of the text fields can be set to short, medium, or long.
- **PROFILE:** Similar to the Likert scale, but it allows you to use a different set of adjectives for each row of scale points.

Answers
Only available if Likert or Profile types are selected.

- **SINGLE ANSWER:** One scale point can be selected per row.
- **MULTIPLE ANSWER:** Multiple scale points can be selected per row. Changes scale points to check boxes.
- **DROP-DOWN LIST:** Places scale points into a drop-down list. This is only single answer.

Options

- **TRANSPOSE TABLE:** If selected, switches the position of the scale points and row statements. Button behavior is reversed as well. Single Answer will only allow one selection per column, as opposed to one selection per row.
- **POSITION TEXT ABOVE:** Places text above the row of buttons, rather than to the side, allowing more room for the scale points. Available for all Matrix Types, except Profile.
- **REPEAT HEADERS:** Repeats the text of the scale points in the middle of the question, at the bottom of the question, or in both positions. Select repeat headers and then specify the location.
- **ADD WHITE SPACE:** Will place additional white space between sets of rows to make the question easier to look at.

Text Entry

Text Entry questions allow respondents to type in verbatim responses, such as comments and contact information (Figure A-3).

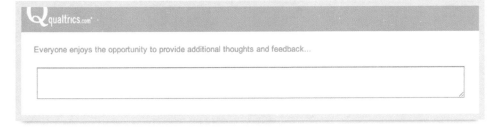

Everyone enjoys the opportunity to provide additional thoughts and feedback...

Figure A-3 Example of Text Entry Multi Line question type.

VARIATIONS OF TEXT ENTRY QUESTION:

- **SINGLE LINE:** The height of a single line and designed for smaller amounts of text.
- **MULTI-LINE:** The height of multiple lines of text and designed for more text.
- **ESSAY TEXT BOX:** The height of multiple lines of text (more than the Multi-Line option) and designed for the maximum amount of text. Useful when prompting respondents to give a lengthy response.
- **FORM:** Allows you to create a form with multiple text entry fields. Typically used when requesting contact information. Can be altered for short, medium, long, and essay size text fields. Allows content validation (numbers only, text only, email address) to be applied to individual rows.
- **PASSWORD:** Similar to the Single Line text entry option, but the entered text appears as an entered password *(example: *****).*

You can choose validation options, such as minimum/maximum character lengths (amount of text characters that can be input in the text field), as well as content validation (valid email address, date, phone, zip code, US State, number, or text). For more information on validation options, check out the Validation section.

While there are different text field sizes for different scenarios, the Qualtrics tool will not restrict the amount of text the respondent can enter. Tools like Excel and SPSS do have character limits regarding the amount of text they can display in their cells, though the latest versions can typically accept large amounts of text.

Text/Graphic

Increase question relevance and respondent involvement by using explanatory text, graphics, or videos.

The Text/Graphic question type allows you to place explanatory or introductory text at the beginning of your survey without having answer choices attached (Figure A-4). It is also useful when inserting images, files, and videos.

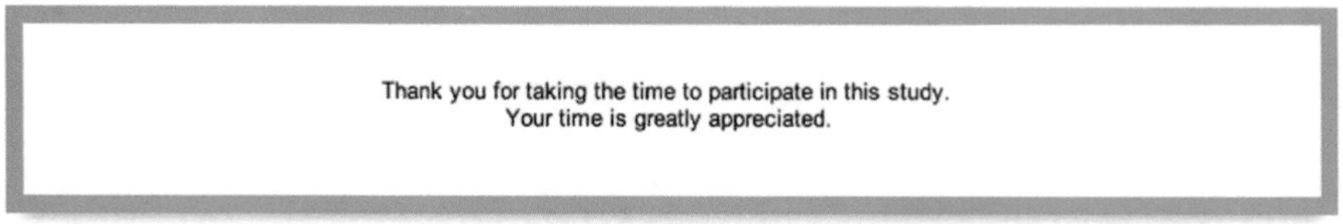

Thank you for taking the time to participate in this study.
Your time is greatly appreciated.

Figure A-4 Example of Text/Graphic question type.

This question type does not have answer choices for a respondent to select, so it is strictly for explanatory or instructional purposes. You can base logic off whether or not the Text/Graphic question type was displayed to the respondent.

The Text/Graphic question type is *not* displayed in the reports, but it does have a column in the data you download from the Download Data page. The data will be marked with a "1" for the respondent if they saw the Text/Graphic question.

Constant Sum

Gather ratio-scaled data based on relative comparisons. Typically used for gathering and summing numeric amounts, like percentages or currency.

The Constant Sum question allows respondents to enter numeric responses, such as what percentage of time, income, or attitudinal preference for particular activities or products. You can specify that the numbers entered must total a certain value (Figure A-5).

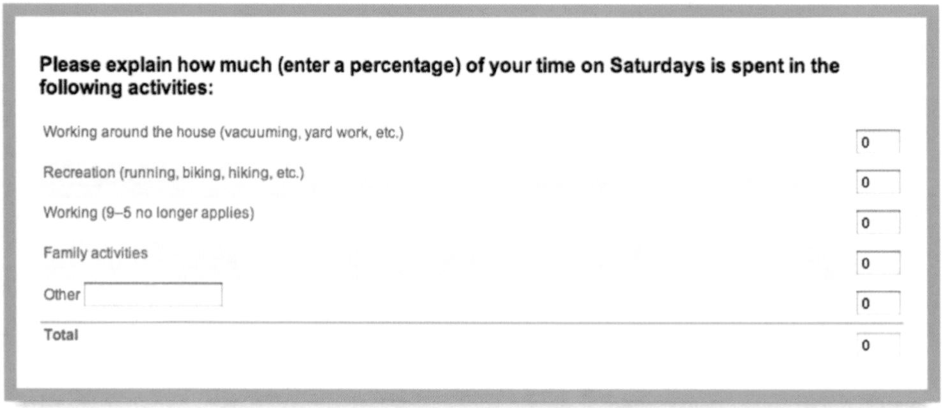

Please explain how much (enter a percentage) of your time on Saturdays is spent in the following activities:

Working around the house (vacuuming, yard work, etc.)	0
Recreation (running, biking, hiking, etc.)	0
Working (9–5 no longer applies)	0
Family activities	0
Other	0
Total	0

Figure A-5 Example of a Constant Sum question type with a Total box.

CONSTANT SUM VARIATIONS:

- **CHOICES:** Allows respondent to type in a value. A Total box can be displayed, and the choices can be displayed vertically or horizontally.
- **BARS:** Displays adjustable bars the respondent slides left to right. You can control how many grid lines, the min/max values, if and how many scale points are displayed, whether the value is displayed to the right of each row, and a custom start position. Commonly used as a more interesting way to gather respondent data.
- **SLIDERS:** Like the Bars, this displays graphical sliders the respondent slides left to right. You can control the number of grid lines, the min/max values, if and how many scale points are displayed, whether a value is displayed to the right of each row, and a custom start position. Commonly used as a more interesting way to gather respondent data.

Slider

A Constant Sum question that's easy to use and full of respondent involvement.

The Slider allows respondents to drag sliders, bars, or stars to express numeric amounts (Figure A-6). This question type is interactive, involving, and attention grabbing. It can be a good alternative to the Matrix Table. This is very similar to the Constant Sum Sliders question type.

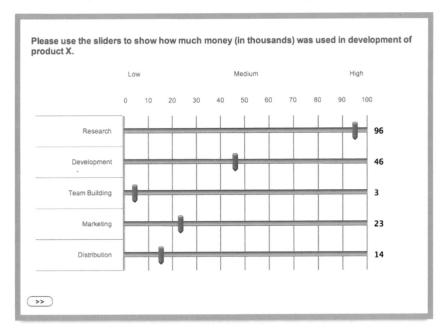

Figure A-6 Example of the Slider question type.

Sliding Scale

Sliding scales graphically express satisfaction or feelings about a particular subject.

The Sliding Scale allows respondents to express themselves using graphical gauges, thermometers, stop-lights, grades, blocks, smiley faces, and more (as shown in Figure A-7).

Please use the slider to the left to express your level of satisfaction with today's customer service experience.

Figure A-7 Example of a Sliding Scale question type with Smiley face graphics.

To find this question type, click the green **Change Question Type** button, click **Show All Question Types**, then scroll to the **Sliding Scale** section.

Rank Order

Asking the respondent to rank ⅓ to ½ of the items in your list in order of preference produces powerful data.

With Rank Order questions, respondents can express their preference for items by ranking or ordering them (Figure A-8). Please note that Rank Order questions do not provide the degree to which the choices differ, only their rank position.

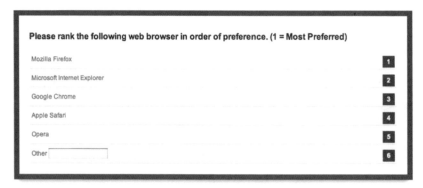

Please rank the following web browser in order of preference. (1 = Most Preferred)

Mozilla Firefox	1
Microsoft Internet Explorer	2
Google Chrome	3
Apple Safari	4
Opera	5
Other	6

Figure A-8 Example of Rank Order Drag and Drop question type.

RANK ORDER VARIATIONS:

- **DRAG AND DROP:** Respondents drag and drop choices into position. Useful for interaction and keeping participants attentive.
- **RADIO BUTTONS:** Allows respondents to rank the statements by clicking on radio buttons. It looks similar to the Matrix Likert question type with slightly different functionality.
- **TEXT BOX:** Allows respondents to rank statements by typing in a number.

Pick, Group, and Rank

Similar to Rank Order, respondents can drop items into a bucket and then rank the items in each bucket according to preference, importance, frequency of purchase, or other measures.

Similar to Rank Order, the Pick, Group, & Rank question type allows respondents to place choices into a group, then rank them within that group (Figure A-9).

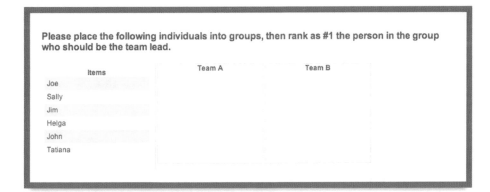

Figure A-9 Example of Pick, Group, and Rank - Drag and Drop question type.

PICK, GROUP, & RANK VARIATIONS:

- **DRAG AND DROP:** Respondents drag and drop the choices into groups and rank them. The groups are defined by the survey builder (like Predefined option).
- **PREDEFINED:** You predefine the groups. Instead of dragging and dropping, the respondent selects the answer choice and clicks an arrow to move the answer choice into the groups you have defined. Once in the group, the respondent uses similar arrows to move the choice up or down to rank it within the group.
- **RECIPIENT DEFINED:** The respondent can specify the names of the groups and amount of groups in the question. Instead of dragging and dropping, the respondent selects the answer choice and clicks an arrow to move the answer choice into the groups they defined. Once in the group, the respondent uses similar arrows to move the choice up or down to rank it within the group.

Side by Side

Consider combining matched questions like importance and performance of a brand on a set of attributes into a side by side matrix format. This focuses attention on the attribute and makes the evaluation tasks easier for respondents to complete.

Side by Side allows you to place multiple Matrix Likert questions next to each other in separate columns (Figure A-10). The row statements are the same across all columns, but the scale is different for each column. Note that each column of the question is displayed in the results as a separate question.

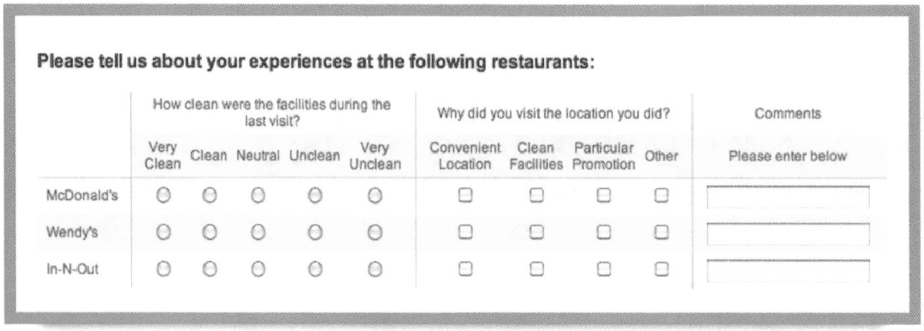
Please tell us about your experiences at the following restaurants:

	How clean were the facilities during the last visit?					Why did you visit the location you did?				Comments
	Very Clean	Clean	Neutral	Unclean	Very Unclean	Convenient Location	Clean Facilities	Particular Promotion	Other	Please enter below
McDonald's	○	○	○	○	○	☐	☐	☐	☐	
Wendy's	○	○	○	○	○	☐	☐	☐	☐	
In-N-Out	○	○	○	○	○	☐	☐	☐	☐	

Figure A-10 Example of Side by Side question type.

SIDE-BY-SIDE VARIATIONS:

Scaled Response

- **DROP-DOWN LIST:** All scale points appear in a drop-down list.
- **SINGLE ANSWER:** Radio buttons are used to allow only one selection.
- **MULTIPLE ANSWER:** Checkboxes are used to allow multiple selections.

Open-Ended Text

- **SHORT:** Short text box length, more suitable for numbers.
- **MEDIUM:** Medium text box length, more suitable for small amounts of text.
- **LONG:** Long text box length, more suitable for larger amounts of text.

To access the options for each Side-by-Side variation, click on the **Column Options** drop-down for each column you have inserted.

Drill Down

Nested multiple choice questions are common when collecting factual data. In specifying a product year, make and model, each selection affects the options available in the next drop-down list.

The Drill Down question type allows respondents to choose an answer option by narrowing down from a general category to a specific category (Figure A-11). In order to achieve this objective you must upload a file (.csv) and provide ALL possible combinations within the different categories.

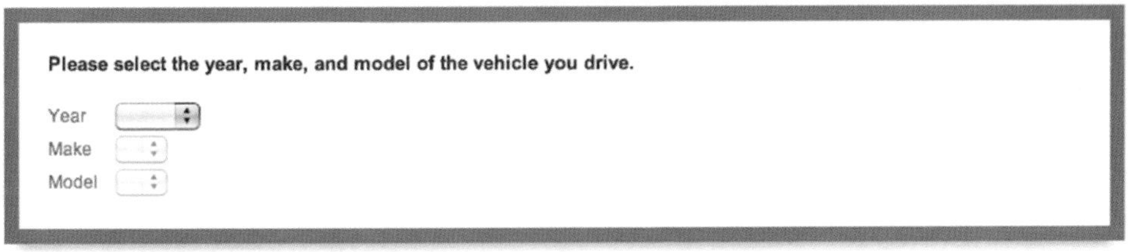

Please select the year, make, and model of the vehicle you drive.

Year
Make
Model

Figure A-11 Example of Drill Down Question.

CREATING THE DRILL DOWN TAKES MULTIPLE STEPS:

1. Form a list of answer choices.
   - An example file is available to you by selecting **Click here to add answers** (after you've inserted the Drill Down question type) and clicking the **Example Document** button on the right side of the dialog window that appears.
2. Create your answer choice selections starting with broad categories and getting more specific. The example below illustrates this (Table A-1).
3. After creating your list, upload it to your survey by clicking **Click here to add answers** in your Drill Down question.

Column 1	Column 2
String	Violin
String	Viola
String	Cello
Woodwind	Flute
Woodwind	Clarinet
Woodwind	Oboe
Brass	Trumpet
Brass	Trombone
Brass	Tuba

Table A-1 Example format for Drill Down question type

In this example, musical instruments are used as answer choice options according to their 1) Name and 2) Type. Column 2 has all the instrument names which respondents are expected to select from. It was created before Column 1 (Instrument Types) for the purpose of easier sorting. Column 1 contains all the instrument types to which Column 2 items correspond.

- Make sure the file you created is saved from Excel or another spreadsheet program as a .csv file (a text file).
- In the **Add Answers to Drill Down** window, make sure the correct **delimiter** is selected under Import Options. Commas are most common, but this can vary depending on the region you live in, so select one of the available options or type the symbol into the text field of the delimiter you are using (";", ":", ".", etc.).

Heat Map

Track interest areas in an ad. Respondents can click anywhere on an image to specify what stands out. The results appear like a representation of heat according to the areas most clicked.

The Heat Map allows you to insert a picture that the respondent can then click on to indicate the area of interest that catches their attention, or that they like the most. In the results, you will be able to see where all the respondents clicked (see Figure A-12).

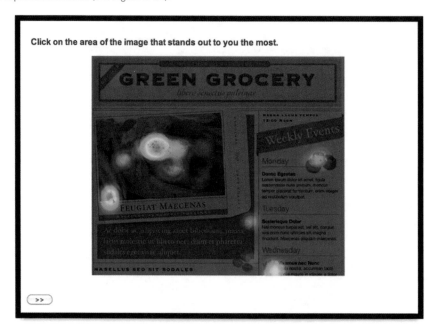

Figure A-12 Example of Heat Map question type and how the results would look.

Hot Spot

Similar to Heat Map, but you define user selectable wire-frame regions of the image.

The Hot Spot question is like the heat map question, but regions of the picture that you want to test (want respondents to click on) are predefined by you (Figure A-13). The respondent clicks on an area to indicate their like or dislike of the predefined region or area. This question type is very useful if you would like to test the effectiveness of a graphic or website.

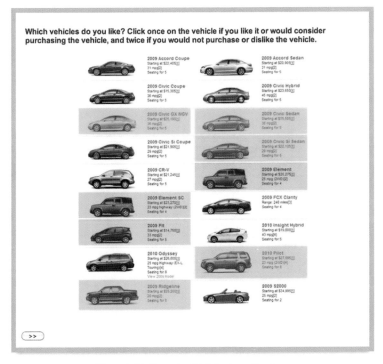

Figure A-13 Example of Hot Spot question type.

HOT SPOT VARIATIONS:

On/Off: Respondents can "turn on" or "turn off" certain areas by clicking.
- Green means the section is **On**.
- No color means the section is **Off**.

Like/Dislike: Respondents can "like" or "dislike" certain areas by clicking once or twice.
- Green means **Like** is selected (one click).
- Red means **Dislike** is selected (two clicks).
- No color means neither **Like** nor **Dislike** is specified.

Gap Analysis

Respondents can rate satisfaction and specify what factors were responsible for this rating.

In some ways similar to the Side-by-Side and Matrix questions, the Gap Analysis allows respondents to rate satisfaction on a five-point smiley face scale, then specify why they selected the rating using the Tell Us Why section (see Figure A-14).

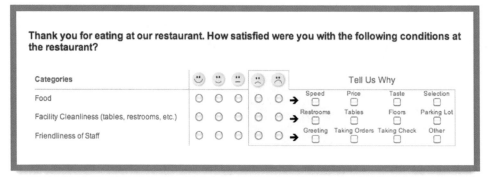

Figure A-14 Example of Gap Analysis Negative question type.

GAP ANALYSIS VARIATIONS:

- **POSITIVE:** The Tell Us Why section is linked to the positive smileys in the scale so respondents can tell what was satisfactory.
- **NEGATIVE:** The Tell Us Why section is linked to the negative smileys in the scale so respondents can tell what was not satisfactory.

File Upload

Have respondents upload a document, image, etc. as part of their survey response.

The File Upload allows respondents to browse their machine and upload a file (document, image, etc.) to their survey response (Figure A-15). The files can be downloaded from the reports one by one or all together as a .zip file.

Please upload a copy of your lesson plan using the text below.

(Choose File) Lecture 2 New Research.pdf

Figure A-15 Example of File Upload.

ALERT: Security measures prevent executable files (.exe, etc.) from being uploaded.

Timing

Useful for experimental design in a survey. Also used to identify cheaters and speeders who produce poor quality data. Track each respondent's time spent answering a particular survey page.

The Timing question is very helpful in conducting experiments and tracking how long a respondent was on a page (Figure A-16). It also allows you to disable the Submit (or Next) button for a specified amount of time, as well as specify an amount of time before automatically advancing the respondent to the next page of the survey. The question is not displayed to respondents and does not prompt a response.

Timing

This page timer will not be displayed to the recipient.
First Click: *24.552 seconds.*
Last Click: *89.614 seconds.*
Page Submit: *0 seconds.*
Click Count: *13 clicks.*

(Close)

Figure A-16 Example of Timing question type data.

The Timing question is valuable because you can see how long respondents were on a page to look at a particular condition. You can see how long someone looks at an image or video and terminate them if they don't view it long enough. You also have control over how long someone looks at a condition. For example, you can force respondents to remain on the page for a certain amount of time and not click right through to the next page. These are powerful tools at your disposal for monitor the quality of your response data.

INFORMATION GATHERED BY TIMING QUESTION:

- **FIRST CLICK:** Amount of time that passed before the respondent's first click on page.
- **LAST CLICK:** Amount of time that passed before respondent's last click on page before clicking the Next (>>) button.
- **PAGE SUBMIT:** Amount of time that passed before respondent clicked Submit/Next button on page.
- **CLICK COUNT:** Total amount of times respondent clicked on the page.

ADDITIONAL FUNCTIONALITY:

- **SECONDS TO DISABLE SUBMIT:** The amount of time in seconds the participant must wait before being able to click the Submit, or Next, button to move to the next page. The button will not show up till the time passes.
- **SECONDS TO AUTO-ADVANCE:** The amount of time in seconds before the participant is automatically moved to the next page of the survey.

Q-TIP

- The timer starts counting once the page finishes loading in the browser.
- The Timing question type is actually a **page timer** and must be added to each page you'd like to time.
- If you want to time a specific question, then separate the actual question along with the Timing question onto one page.
- The timer collects time to the millisecond.
- This question is not displayed to respondents, though it is shown under Survey Preview mode for testing purposes. Select "Do Not Show Hidden Questions" to not display in preview mode.
- Logic can be based off the Timing question counts.
- **Seconds to disable submit** and **Seconds to auto-advance** can be used in conjunction.

Meta Info Question

The Meta Info question type collects information on how the respondent is accessing your survey (Figure A-17). This is great for feedback surveys, especially on websites where it would be useful to know the operating system and web browser they use. This question type is not seen by the respondent.

Find out the browser and operating system information your respondents are using when taking your survey. Useful in technology surveys, and can be useful to know if most respondents are using Windows, Mac, or a mobile device.

Figure A-17 Meta Info from an iPhone/iPod Touch (from the Survey Preview link).

INFORMATION GATHERED BY THE META INFO QUESTION:

- **BROWSER:** Browser name (MSIE, Firefox, Chrome, Safari).
- **VERSION:** Version of the browser they're running (like 8.0, 5.0.3).
- **OPERATING SYSTEM:** Specifies if running Windows or Mac, or another operating system (Windows NT 6.1, Intel Mac OS X 10_6_6).
- **SCREEN RESOLUTION:** Resolution of the respondent's monitor (1920x1080).
- **FLASH VERSION:** Version of Adobe Flash running on the respondent's machine. If Flash is not installed, a "-1" displays (like for the iPhone/iPad).
- **JAVA SUPPORT:** Shows if Java is installed on respondent's machine. "1" means Java installed, "0" means it is not.
- **USER AGENT:** Every browser has a user agent string that tells a website what it is, and typically what engine it is using to display its content.

Appendix B
Polls

A Poll is a nice way to make your website interactive.
Qualtrics will generate the HTML for you to put into your website.
It will display a simple poll question and provide the results
whenever a respondent answers it.

Polls

Polls are a great tool for checking the pulse of your site visitors (Figure B-1). You can put up a poll for fun or request more serious feedback. Because they are just one-question, they don't allow for the same reporting options as surveys, but they can still gather valuable information.

If you're going to use a poll, make sure you don't need the ability to download the data or generate reports. A poll will only provide the basic question and the ability to show results.

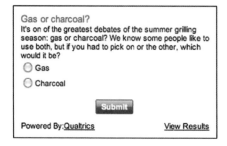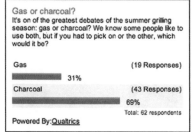

Figure B-1 Sample Poll.

In the Polls tab, your polls display in a list on the left, and are edited in a blue column of options on the right (Figure B-2).

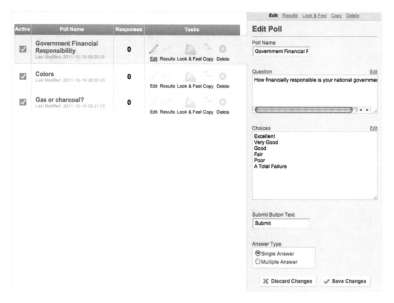

Figure B-2 Create a Poll.

TO CREATE A NEW POLL:

1. On the *Polls* tab, click the **Create Poll** button near the top of the page.
2. Use the various directions below to make changes to your poll. Make sure to click the **Save Changes** button as you go.
3. When finished, click the green **Add This Poll to Your Website** button to get the JavaScript code necessary to post the poll on your website or blog.

TO EDIT A POLL:

1. Click the **Edit** task icon next to your poll.
2. Type a name for your poll in the Poll Name field.
3. In the Question field, enter the question text you want to ask. Click **Edit** to use the Rich Content Editor.
4. In the Choices field, enter one answer choice per line. Click **Edit** to use the Rich Content Editor.
5. In the Submit Button Text field, feel free to change the button's text. The default is "Submit".
6. In the Answer Type field, specify if you want Single Answer (radio buttons) or Multiple Answer (checkboxes).
7. Click **Save Changes**.

TO VIEW THE RESULTS:

1. Click the **Results** task icon next to your poll. This will display the bar graph of responses. This is the same view your poll respondents will see after answering.

Click **Reset Poll** to remove existing responses. Since this removes the response data, you will be prompted to confirm the reset.

TO EDIT THE LOOK AND FEEL OF YOUR POLL:

1. Click the **Look & Feel** task icon next to your poll. You will see your poll and a list of options below it. This is similar to the survey Look and Feel section on the *Edit Survey* tab.
   - **COLORS:** Click the color square on the right side to change the color for any of the listed items. You can change the following items:
     - **BACKGROUND:** The entire background of the poll.
     - **TITLE:** The poll title color. This displays by default. You can tell it not to display under the General section.
     - **QUESTION:** The question text color.
     - **CHOICES:** The answer choice color.
     - **BUTTON TEXT:** The submit button text color.
     - **RESULTS BAR:** This refers to the bars in the graph used to display the results.

- **SIZE:** Change the size of the poll and the associated text and results bars.
    - **TITLE, QUESTION, AND CHOICES:** Use the drop-down menu to specify your preferred text size.
    - **POLL WIDTH:** Enter the size of the poll. By default it uses pixels (px), but you can also place a percent.
    - **RESULTS BAR THICKNESS:** Use pixels to adjust the size of the bars in the bar graph.
- **FONT:** Use the drop-down menu to change the font of the entire poll.
- **BUTTON:** Choose one of twelve color schemes to customize how your button looks.
- **GENERAL:** Make some basic changes to your poll.
    - **SHOW TITLE:** Specify if you want to show your poll's title. This is selected by default.
    - **ALLOW RESULTS TO BE VIEWED WITHOUT VOTING:** A site visitor can click the View Results button on the poll to view the results without having responded to the poll first. This is enabled by default.
    - **ALLOW A USER TO VOTE MULTIPLE TIMES:** A site visitor can answer the poll more than once. This is not selected by default.
    - **SORT RESULTS:** This will sort the results in Ascending or Descending order (you choose) according to which choices were selected most often. So the most frequently selected choice can always be displayed at the top or bottom of the list of choices in the bar graph.
- **ADVANCED:** This gives you an Edit CSS button. Clicking the button will give you a lot of CSS styles you can use to further customize your poll. This is advanced because you will want to make sure you have CSS/HTML familiarity before jumping in.
2. Remember to click the **Save Changes** button before moving on.

TO COPY A POLL:

1. Just click the **Copy** task icon next to the poll you want to copy. An exact replica will be placed in your list of polls, which you can edit as needed.

TO DELETE A POLL:

1. Click the **Delete** task icon next to the poll.
2. Select **Delete Poll** to the right to confirm deletion.

ALERT: All data associated with the poll will be deleted as well.

Q - T I P

- Many pages have a **Discard Changes** button at the bottom. Click this to remove any changes you have made before saving.
- If you know someone that wants to use a poll, but doesn't have an account with Qualtrics, send them to **Pollmo.com**. Pollmo.com is powered by Qualtrics. It gives you many of the same polling features of Qualtrics, but doesn't require an account to use it.

Classic Reporting

Building a report can be intimidating. The View Results has many research tools that can help you whip your data into shape. Make your data into a report, analyze it, then share it with your colleagues, all from one location.

View Results tab is where you go when you want to view and analyze the data you've collected. You can view and edit a report, cross-tabulate the data, view the individual responses, and download the data to an external application. The classic reporting is slowly getting phased out. If you want information on the latest reporting tools available in the Qualtrics Survey Research Suite, please check out chapter 9.

Figure 9-1 *View Results tab and available reporting options.*

You will see Surveys Started and Surveys Completed counts on the View Results pages. These counts only include closed survey sessions, unlike the Surveys Started count found on the Email History page. **Surveys Started** includes both completed surveys and partially completed surveys due to partial data. **Surveys Completed** just counts completed responses (those that passed over an End Survey element in the survey).

View Reports

Generate custom charts and tables about your data with the click of your mouse.

The View Reports page is where you generate a report and view tables and graphs for each question in your survey.

The first time you go to the View Reports page, you will see the **Select a Report** view. The Qualtrics Survey Research Suite has automatically generated the **Initial Report** for you. Click the Initial Report to view it or click **Create a New Report** to load a completely new report. In this view, you can also delete a report by clicking its corresponding **Delete button** to the right.

Let's click **Create a New Report** and load a new report.

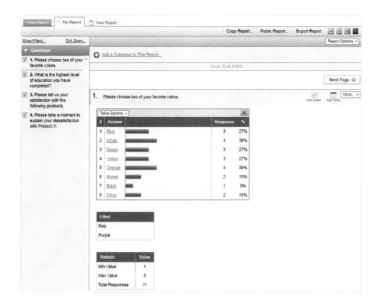

Figure 9-2 A report loaded on the View Reports page.

There are quite a few reporting tools to be aware of. See Figure 9.2 for reference.

- **REPORT TABS:** As you create reports, the tabs for your reports will show up at the top of the reporting page. Click the tab for the report you want to load or click New Report to create a new one. You will be prompted to give it a name first. After naming the report, click the green check mark.
- **QUESTIONS:** The questions are listed in the blue column on the left.
  - Click the question's text to jump directly to it.
  - Click the space next to the question and drag it to a new position in the question order.
  - Uncheck the box to not display a question in the report.
    - Shift+click a checkbox to select or uncheck all questions in the list. This is useful if there are a lot of questions that need to be shown or not shown in the report.
- **TABLES AND GRAPHS:** In the main body of the report is where you view the tables and graphs.
  - Graphs are not inserted automatically.

GRAPHS

Many graph types are available to best represent your data.

Graphs, also known as charts, are a great way to visually display your data. Various graph types are available, allowing you to find just the right way to show the responses. You can choose between vertical and horizontal bar charts, pie charts, line graphs, and even radar graphs. Please note graphs are **not** automatically inserted into reports and must be inserted manually.

To insert a graph for a question:

1. Click **Add Graph** at the top right of the question area.

To remove a graph for a question:
  1. Hover over the graph you want to remove.
  2. Click the X that appears at the top right of the graph.

To change the style of graph displayed:
  1. Hover over the graph.
  2. Hover over the style of graph.
  3. Click the specific style or variation you prefer.

GRAPH OPTIONS

Graph Options are found by hovering over the graph and clicking the Graph Options button near the top left of the graph.

- **DATA SOURCE:** Choose between the question's Count, Percent, and Mean to generate the graph. Count is the default.
- **SORT BY:** Sort the graph by Answer choice text (alphabetically), Response count, or None at all. None is the default.
- **SHOW VALUES:** Toggle on/off the display of the graph value. The value displayed is determined by the Data Source selection.
- **TRUNCATE LABELS:** Designed for questions with long choice text, you can truncate, or shorten, the choice text to allow more space for the rest of the graph.
- **GRAPH RENDERER:** Toggle whether the graph is displayed using an Image or Flash. Flash includes some animation when the graph is generated and when hovering over it. Flash requires the flash plug-in be installed on the browser. Image is the default.
- **DECIMALS:** Show between 0 and 3 decimal places. This only applies when using Show Values and the selected Data Source option has decimals (like Percent and Mean).
- **SHOW/HIDE COLUMNS:** Toggle on/off choices to display or not display in the graph.
- **EXPORT GRAPH TO:** Export the graph as an image to Word, Powerpoint, or PDF formats.
- **REMOVE GRAPH:** Remove the graph from the report. This is the same as hovering over the graph and clicking the X, as described earlier.

TABLES

Simple numeric and percentage tables list your answer choices and show the basic information.

Tables are a great way to show a lot of information in not a lot of space. By default for most question types, a table will display the answer choice, its answer choice value, the number of times it was selected (Responses), its percentage of times selected, and even integrate a simple horizontal bar chart. There are various table types from the standard table type, statistics table, and the text entry table.

To insert a table for a question:
  1. Click **Add Table** at the top right of the question area.

To remove a table for a question:
    1. Hover over the table you want to remove.
    2. Click the X that appears at the top right of the table.

To add a Statistics table or Text Entry table:
    1. Click **More** button at top right of question area.
    2. Select **Add Statistics** table or **Add Text Entry table**, as needed.

TABLE OPTIONS

Table Options are found by hovering over the table and clicking the Table Options button near the top left of the table.

- **SORT BY:** Sort the table display by selecting one of the table header options, like # (choice value), Answer, Bar, Response, or %. This can also be done by clicking directly on the desired table header on the table itself.
- **DECIMALS:** Show between 0 and 3 decimal places in the % column. The default is 0.
- **SHOW/HIDE COLUMNS:** Toggle on/off the display of the table's columns.
- **SHOW/HIDE ROWS:** Toggle on/off the display of the table's rows (answer choices, etc.).
- **EXPORT TABLE TO:** Export the table to Word, Powerpoint, Excel (.csv), and PDF formats.

NOTES

Add text to your report to point out a result, trend, or interesting implication.

Notes allow you to leave a short, informative message for anyone who might be viewing the report.

To insert a Note:
    1. Click **More** button at top right of question area.
    2. Select **Add Note**.

To edit a Note:
    1. Click in the text area of note.
    2. Start entering your text.

To format a Note's text:
    1. Click in the text area of the note.
    2. Click the **blue arrow** button to right of text area.
    3. Select **Rich Content Editor**. You can now use the editor to format the text of the note.

FILTERS

Filters are how you can slice and dice your data to see how particular demographics of your data answered the survey. You can filter by subgroup, question text, Date Range, and Completion Status.

To find the filters area of the report, click the **Show Filters** button at the top left of the blue questions column at the left of the report.

While filters are applied in different ways, they all display as a red label at the top of the report and can be removed in the same way.

To remove a filter applied to a report:
1. Click the **X** on the red label at the top of the report. The report will reload with that filter no longer applied.

QUESTION SEARCH

The Question Search filter is useful for finding a particular question when you have a large survey with a lot of questions.

To use the Question Search filter:
1. Click the **Question Search** field.
2. Type question text to start searching through the question text.

DATE RANGE

The Date Range filter allows you to filter the data according to absolute and relative date ranges.

To apply a Date Range filter:
1. Click the **Date Range** drop-down menu (All Dates is the default selection).
2. Select an option.
   a. Select a preset relative option. You can choose a predefined amount of days, a month, or a quarter.
   b. Click **Custom** to apply an absolute date range. Click the Calendar icon next to the From and To fields to specify that field.

COMPLETION STATUS
The Completion Status filter is a way to filter and only view the completed responses or partial responses.

To apply a Completion Status filter:
1. Click the **Completion Status** column.
2. Select **Completed** or **Partial**.

SUBGROUPS

Subgroups are the most commonly used filter in a Qualtrics report. You can filter on question selection and embedded data field.

To set up a subgroup filter:
1. In the filters area, click the **New** button on the **Subgroup** header.
2. Specify what to filter on.
   a. If **Question**, follow the prompts. While each question type will be slightly different, most will be similar to the following:
      i. Select the question to reference in the filter.
      ii. Select the answer choice.
      iii. Specify if you want to filter on whether the choice is **Selected** or **Not Selected**.
   b. If **Embedded Data** is selected, follow the prompts:
      i. Enter the Embedded Data **Field Name**.
      ii. Specify how you want to interact with the embedded data value.
      iii. Enter the Embedded Data **Value**.
3. Click **Save Subgroup**.

To Edit an existing subgroup filter:
1. In the filters area, click to expand the Subgroups heading.
2. Hover over the subgroup and click **Edit**.

To Delete an existing subgroup filter:
1. In the filters area, click to expand the Subgroups heading.
2. Hover over the subgroup and click **Edit**.
3. Click **Delete Subgroup** at the bottom left of the subgroup window.

- Set up a quick subgroup filter by clicking **Add a Subgroup to This Report** at the top of the report.
- To name a subgroup you've set up for easy reference later on, when editing the subgroup, click **Rename** at the top of the filter.

RESPONSE SETS

Response Sets are a way to set up different data collection buckets. You can edit your Response Sets under Survey Options on the Edit Survey tab. The topic is also discussed further under Survey Options in chapter 3 of this book.

To set up a Response Set filter:
1. Click to expand the Response Set heading.
2. Click on a Response Set to reload the report with just that Response Set's data.

- In most cases a Response Set is not necessary to use.
- Only one Response Set can be viewed at a time. If wanting to view more than one at a time, you will need to export the data from the different Response Sets, then import it into the same survey.

DRILL DOWN

Similar to a very simple cross tabulation, drilling down on a question allows you to view a comparison of one question to every other question in the report.

To set up a Drill Down:

1. Navigate to the question you want to Drill Down on.
2. Click the **Drill Down** button at the top right of the blue questions column to the left of the report.
3. A window will display confirming you want to Drill Down on that question. Click **OK** to confirm. The report will reload with your Drill Down applied.

- If you are displaying multiple questions per page in the report, clicking Drill Down will display a light blue highlight that follows your mouse. Move your mouse over the question where you want to apply the Drill Down and click to apply.
- If selecting a Matrix Table, you will be given the ability to highlight a particular row of the Matrix Table to drill down on.

REPORT OPTIONS

Report Options allow you to apply some general options to the entire report.

MAKE REPORT PUBLIC

Sharing results is good. Turn your report into a web page anyone can view, or selectively share by using password protection.

This is the same as clicking the Public Report button on the gray bar across the top of the report. A Public Report is a very useful way to share a report with multiple parties interested in the results. It turns your report into a web page, giving you a URL you can provide them to click and view the report with the most up-to-date data.

To set up a Public Report:

1. Click the **Public Report** button. A window will appear.
2. Click **Turn On Public Report** button.
3. **Copy** Public Report URL and provide as needed. Most people email this to those interested or provide URL on a website for general viewing.

To turn off a Public Report:

1. Click the **Public Report** button.
2. Click **Turn Off Public Report** button.

- For more security, select **Enable Password Protection**. You are then prompted to enter a **password** and click the **Save Password** button when finished. Anyone attempting to view the report will be prompted to enter the password before accessing the report.
- Many people using password protection email the report URL and the report password in separate emails for additional security.
- If you are familiar with CSS (Cascading Style Sheets), feel free to click **Custom CSS** to enter your own CSS and edit the look and feel of the report.

SCHEDULE REPORT EMAIL

Schedule Report Email lets you schedule an email to someone on a weekly or monthly basis that includes one of the report export options (PDF, Word, Excel, or Powerpoint document).

Automatically email stakeholders a periodic report of results.

To schedule a report email:

1. Under **Report Options**, click **Schedule Report Email**.
    - If you have previously created a Report Email, click **Add Scheduled Report Email** at the top left of the window.
2. Specify who will receive the Report Email under the **To** section.
3. Click the gray **Please Select** button.
4. Select **Enter Email Addresses** to manually provide the email addresses of those to receive the Report Email. Or if you have a panel of people imported into the tool, hover over the library and find the panel or panel member to select.
5. In the **When** area specify the day and time of day you want the Report Email to be sent on a weekly or monthly basis.
6. Under **Message**, you can specify the details of the message.
    a. **FROM NAME:** This will be piped in from the name on your user account, but can be edited if you need to send it on behalf of a supervisor, etc.
    b. **REPLY-TO EMAIL ADDRESS:** If someone receiving the Report Email clicks Reply, they will reply to this email address. This will be piped from the email address on your user account, but can be edited if you need to send it on behalf of a supervisor, etc.
    c. **SUBJECT:** The subject line of the email.
    d. **ATTACHMENT:** Choose if you want to send the report as a PDF, Word, Excel, or Powerpoint document.
    e. **MESSAGE BODY:** Enter the body of the message or choose an existing message by clicking the **Select a message** button. If you create a new message or edit an existing one, you will be prompted to use the **Save** or **Save As** buttons to save the message text.
7. Click **Save** to schedule the Report Email.

To delete an existing Report Email:

1. Under **Report Options**, click **Schedule Report Email**.
2. Click the **red minus button** to the left of the Report Email in the left column.
3. Click **Save** at the bottom of the window.

- Click **Send Test Email** to send a report email to an email address you specify.
- To send a Report Email more frequently than once per week or month, click the **Add Scheduled Report Email** button at the left of the Schedule Report Email window and repeat the scheduling process.

RENAME REPORT

Select Rename Report to, you guessed it, rename the report to a more descriptive name.

To rename a report:
1. Under **Report Options** select **Rename Report**.
2. A text box will open on the report's tab. Type the new report name.
3. Click the **green checkmark** to save the new report name.

TIME SERIES

Time Series can be used to compare data across two different Response Sets.

To set up Time Series:
1. Under **Report Options** select **Time Series**.
2. Click the **add** button to create as many entries as response sets you will be comparing.
3. Click the gray drop down menus to select the corresponding Response Set for each entry in the Time Series.
4. Using the text boxes on the left side, enter a label for each Response Set used in the Time Series.
5. When finished, click **Save**.

To insert Time Series Graphs and Tables:
1. Find the question in the report where you would like a Time Series Table or Graph.
2. Click the **More** drop-down menu.
3. Select either **Add Time-Series Table** or **Add Time-Series Graph**.

To change the order of Response Sets in the Time Series view, click and drag the **Move** button next to the Response Set.

QUESTIONS PER PAGE

By default, reports load with one question per page. Hovering over Questions per Page allows you to choose how many questions per page you want your report to load. You can choose as few as one (the default) or as many as 50.

QUESTION NUMBERING

Question Numbering allows you to change how the questions are numbered in the report. You can choose between None (no numbering), Sequential (the default), and Export Tag (uses the Q# code seen on the Edit Survey page).

REORDER REPORT

Reorder Report opens a window with an interface designed to make it easier to change the order of questions in the report.

To reorder questions in report:

1. Under **Report Options**, click **Reorder Report**.
2. **Click question** to select it. Or click and drag over multiple questions to select more than one. When selected questions will highlight blue.
3. Use the buttons to the right to move the questions up one spot, down one spot, or all the way to the top or bottom.
4. When finished, click **Save**.

- If concerned about questions in the report not displaying in the same order as they appear on the Edit Survey tab, try creating a new report. This recreates the report with the questions in the same order as they currently appear under Edit Survey.
- While the Reorder Report interface makes it easier for large changes in question order, question order can also be changed by clicking and dragging individual questions in the regular question column view.

DECIMAL PLACES

The Decimal Places option allows you to choose if percentages in the report display 0, 1, 2, or 3 decimal places.

MATRIX VALUES

Matrix Values lets you specify if Matrix questions in your report display their data with Percentages or Counts. The default is Counts.

GRAPH COLORS

Graph Colors lets you adjust the color scheme used for your report's graphs. You can click any of the color squares to adjust the color palette used.

TOGGLE STRETCH MODE

Stretch Mode stretches the tables to the full width of the browser page. The default mode is a fixed view that adjusts the width of the table according to the number of choices.

DELETE REPORT

Select this option to completely delete the report. You will be prompted to confirm the report's deletion.

COPY REPORT

Do you have a report set up just right and don't want to redo all your work on another report? If so, copy your report and you won't have to start over from scratch.

To copy a report:
1. Click the **Copy Report** button at the top of the report.
2. Enter a name for the new report.
3. Click **Save**.

EXPORT REPORT

*Need an
exportable
report in
PDF, Word,
Powerpoint, or
Excel format?
No Problem.*

Under Export Report you can export a copy of your report as a file in PDF, Word, Powerpoint, or Excel (.csv) formats. Just click the icon of the desired format.

If you have Microsoft Office 2003 installed on your machine, you will need to install a Compatibility Pack from Microsoft so you can correctly display the file formats for Word and Powerpoint. When you click the link for Word or Powerpoint, Qualtrics provides a link to the Compatibility Pack in the yellow box that displays.

STYLE EDITOR

*Change report
displays by
adding different
colors, font, font
size, and font
color on your
graphs.*

The Style Editor allows you to make some basic changes to how the report displays. You can expand the Style Editor by clicking **Show Style Editor** just below the "Add a Subgroup to This Report" button at the top of the report.

The Style Editor allows you to select Graph Colors (similar to the Graph Colors option under Report Options), change the font and font size, as well as the font color of the entire report.

- To display Embedded Data in the reports, the embedded data field names need to be added to the Survey Flow. Check out the Embedded Data section of chapter 5 for additional information.
- Remember, the Text/Graphic question type won't display in the reports. There are no answers to report on.
- Sometimes questions are out of order, especially with the Initial Report. This happens because the report was automatically created while you were still editing your survey (adding, moving, and/or deleting questions). New questions are placed at the end of existing reports. Just create a new report to get the order you see on the Edit Survey tab.

Qualtrics also provides a Stats window with some additional overall survey statistics. It isn't part of the reporting, but is found by clicking the Stats button directly below the Surveys Started and Surveys Completed counts. These stats can be filtered by date and exported to PDF.

- **SURVEY DURATIONS:** How long people take to complete the survey (hh:mm).
- **SURVEY START TIMES:** Shows the times of day respondents started the survey.
- **SURVEY START DATES:** Shows dates respondents started the survey.
- **QUESTION RESPONSE RATES:** Lists survey questions and shows what percentage of respondents completed that particular question.
- **SURVEY COMPLETION PERCENT:** How much of the survey respondents completed by increments of 10%.

How to Use Qualtrics

Handbook for
Research Professionals

2nd Edition

Official Training Guide from Qualtrics